Peer Mediation

Peer Mediation

Hilary Cremin

Open University Press

Open University Press
McGraw-Hill Education
McGraw-Hill House
Shoppenhangers Road
Maidenhead
Berkshire
England
SL6 2QL

email: enquiries@openup.co.uk
world wide web: www.openup.co.uk

and Two Penn Plaza, New York, NY 10121–2289, USA

First published 2007

A catalogue record of this book is available from the British Library

ISBN   13: 978 0335 221 110 (pb) 978 0335 221 127 (pb)
ISBN   10: 0335 221 114 (hb) 0335 221 122 (hb)

Library of Congress Cataloguing-in-Publication Data
CIP data applied for

Typeset by YHT Ltd, London
Printed in Poland by OZGraf S.A.
www.polskabook.pl

The McGraw·Hill Companies

This book is dedicated to the memory of Jerry Tyrell, whose work in the field of peer mediation in Northern Ireland was cut short so tragically.

Contents

Acknowledgements

There are many people whose ideas have inspired me to write this book. There are many others whose support has been so valuable. They are too numerous to name. A few names, however, must be mentioned. The field of mediation, and peer mediation in particular, is one in which people tend to support each other, share ideas, and build on each other's work. It is certainly the case that my early work on mediation built on the work of the Kingston Friends Workshop Group, and other early pioneers of the field. The Religious Society of Friends (Quakers) have provided quiet support for conflict resolution in schools for decades, and funded much of my early work. Barbara Maines and George Robinson helped me to publish my work on peer mediation for the first time. I would like to acknowledge Rosie Norwood and Cath Barker for keeping Catalyst going whilst I went back into university life, and I would also like to acknowledge the significant role played by Pat Robinson when she joined me as co-director of Catalyst for a number of years.

More specifically, I would like to acknowledge the information on mediation in legal settings provided by Trevor Buck, and the joint work with Keith Faulkes, that fed into much of Chapter 3. Keith Stacey provided support with the reference section, and Gary Thomas helped by reading early drafts.

Last but not least, thanks to all of those who have taught me so much about conflict resolution – even when the lessons were hard. Thanks to Gary, Christie and Fionn for far more than words could ever say.

1   Introduction

Mediation has an important role to play in resolving disputes across the full range of human interaction and discourse – at the levels of interpersonal, organizational, citizen/state, and between-state engagement. Its recent expansion in all of these spheres means that it has the potential to become a significant component in policy initiatives in the procedures of youth justice, family law, probation, education, etc. The way in which mediation is theorized and adopted within different professions will therefore have far-reaching implications. The focus of this book is education; and citizenship education in particular. Of interest here are the ways in which peer mediation can be either embraced or neglected by schools. It can be used to strengthen student voice, student-centred discipline, active citizenship, and inclusion, or else it can fail to achieve these aims, resulting in disillusioned students, and teachers who revert to authoritarian methods of behaviour management, surveillance and control. What are the factors that influence these different outcomes? What methods can be used to gather more information about peer mediation? This book responds to these questions. It is based on my research and work in the field of peer mediation over a period of 17 years, and on an international review of research in this area, including some primary research that is presented here through two case studies.

I have been involved in developing peer mediation since 1990, when I became the coordinator of the West Midlands Peace Education Project (WMQPEP). My work for this charity involved researching peer mediation, particularly in the US, and developing programmes for students in the UK. This work has been continued by WMQPEP, as well as through my company (Catalyst Conflict and Change) established in 1993. Much of this work was based on a peer mediation handbook for teachers (Stacey and Robinson, 1997) written with Pat Robinson, and a video and handbook (Stacey, 2001). My PhD investigated the impact of peer mediation on levels of bullying, self-esteem and empowerment in three primary schools in Birmingham, UK. I am now involved in researching citizenship education, and initial teacher training at the University of Leicester.

Given the above, it might be expected that the book would be uncritical, and perhaps overenthusiastic about mediation, but in fact the reverse may well be the case. Seventeen years is rather a long time for frustrations and disappointments to be reinforced! This is not to deny peer mediation's shining success stories, nor the potential that it still has for supporting current UK policy initiatives such as Every Child Matters (ECM), Personalized learning and Excellence and Enjoyment. Indeed, I am as enthusiastic as ever about the transformative power of mediation. It is merely to point out that the book will provide an overview of the inhibiting factors, as well as the enabling factors, which determine the possibilities for peer mediation in schools. This book draws on my professional experience and insights, but is careful to locate itself as fundamentally driven by research, both my research, and that of others working in this field.

Whilst maintaining the centrality of peer mediation throughout, this book explores areas such as mediation more generally, citizenship education, inclusion and the voice of the child. Key themes, such as empowerment, student-centred approaches, active and participatory pedagogy and an ethic of care emerge in all chapters, as do their nemeses: neoliberalism, authoritarianism and social exclusion. All paths lead back to peer mediation, however, and each chapter contains an overview of research into peer mediation pertaining to the themes of the chapter in question. The final chapter provides a review of research into peer mediation more generally, both an overview of findings, and a critique of methods used. The book ends with recommendations about how research into peer mediation might be developed in the future.

Chapter 2 looks at how mediation is practised in legal, community and education settings. It charts the growth of mediation, alternative dispute resolution (ADR) and restorative justice. It reviews four 'stories' of mediation that are proposed by Baruch Bush and Folger (2005): the satisfaction story; the social justice story; the transformation story and the oppression story. Each of these is linked with a particular tradition of mediation, the first and last being primarily concerned with law. It is suggested in this chapter that mediation, and ADR in general, have grown in the legal sector because of dissatisfaction with litigation and formal processes of law, which are often seen as distant and disempowering. The 'satisfaction story' of mediation is contrasted with the 'transformation story', the latter being proactive and all-encompassing. Transformative mediation changes the nature of conflictual relations, empowering disputants with new perspectives and skills, and providing opportunities for growth and renewal. It is linked with community mediation and mediation in schools, which are both seen as sharing a theoretical underpinning with Rogerian counselling, group facilitation and humanistic education. Chapter 2 goes on to provide perspectives on mediation from psychology and philosophy, some of which are drawn from traditional cultures from the global East and South, before focusing on peer support and peer mediation in schools. Finally, my research investigating the factors behind the success of peer mediation in 15 schools in Birmingham is reviewed, and conclusions are discussed. This includes findings from a group interview with teachers from these schools, and an analysis of the features that these services have in common, such as student empowerment, a whole-school approach, support from senior management, a budget and resources, systems of choice, rewards and incentives for the peer mediators, and conflict-resolution skills training for all students in school. Student attitudes towards mediation and conflict resolution in schools are also discussed.

Chapter 3 focuses on citizenship education in schools. Citizenship is seen as a fragile and contested notion that has much to gain from active and participative education and peer mediation in schools. A historical perspective on citizenship and citizenship education in the UK is given, starting with Marshall's welfare rights, continuing with Thatcher and neoliberalism, and ending with new Labour. New Labour's 'third way' for citizenship education is critiqued, and various political factors that militate against the effective implementation of citizenship education are given, including: policies on parental choice; marketization and private finance of schools; masculinist and statist notions of citizenship in the National Curriculum; and 'yobbery' amongst senior politicians and others. International perspectives on challenges for citizenship education are given, including the demise of peace education, and the concomitant feminized values of care, non-violent action, and local concern for global issues. Potential solutions include the need to create new public spaces in which young people can respond to the decentralization of political power, as well as a reinvention of peace education, grounded in feminized notions of care and interconnections between private and public spheres of life. The chapter ends by giving examples of initiatives such as Every Child Matters (ECM) distributed leadership and student consultation as ways of providing fertile ground for successful citizenship education and peer mediation. The findings from my research into peer mediation in three primary schools in Birmingham are given, and discussed in terms of the need to establish a culture of consultation and empowerment in order for citizenship and peer mediation to thrive.

Chapter 4 looks at issues of inclusion for children with special educational needs (SEN), particularly those with social emotional and behavioural difficulties (SEBD), and the role that peer mediation can play in this. It reviews the shift from medical to environmental models of special educational needs (SEN) and the financial and practical challenges that teachers face in providing inclusive classrooms for all (Thomas and Vaughan, 2004). It is suggested that, despite the difficulties, teachers can and should consult with students with SEBD in order to maintain the health of schools as organizations. Behaviour management that is grounded in student-centred discipline and peer mediation enables student voices to be heard, rather than suppressed and marginalized. This is contrasted with authoritarian and behaviourist methods of discipline, which centre on teacher surveillance and control, denying students opportunities for developing self discipline and a personal moral code, and denying schools opportunities for self-review, growth and renewal (Rogers and Freiberg, 1994). It suggests that authoritarian and behaviourist methods, with the paraphernalia of stickers, stamps, detentions slips, warnings and consequences should not be used to shore up a shoddy test-driven curriculum. Developmental psychology is reviewed, as is the need for schools to be proactive in ensuring that young people develop socio-cognitive skills. Peer mediation is seen as an important strategy for helping to bring this about. The chapter ends by reviewing research into the implementation of peer mediation in a school for students with moderate learning difficulties (Warne, 2003) and the parts of my research that relate to the impact of peer mediation on student-centred discipline.

Chapter 5 looks at student voice, emerging children's rights and a new sociology of childhood (James, Jenks and Prout, 2005) which sees children as social actors, shaping, as well as shaped, by their environment. It reviews 'child panic' and duality in attitudes towards childhood, with children seen as both in need of protection, and as aggressors from whom adults need to be protected. These issues are related back to schools and to peer mediation. Schools are seen as places in which young people have less autonomy than elsewhere, and Ruddock and Flutter's (2004) 'five advocacies' for engaging with student voice are discussed. It is argued more generally that a command-and-control culture within the education sector as a whole militates against processes of consultation, whether these processes involve students or teachers. Teachers are unlikely to empower and consult with students if they feel that their own perspectives are marginalized, and students are unlikely to take consultation seriously if they see that teachers have little power to implement change. Circle time is given as a case in point, with Taylor's (2003) research used to provide examples of the ways in which some teachers find it hard to let go of power and control, even during an activity that is supposed to be empowering for students. My research is revisited to explore similar themes, and research by Sellman (2002) and Bickmore (2001) is reviewed in order to explore the values and practices that underpin the successful implementation of peer mediation.

Chapter Six contains a case study of peer mediation in Stanville Primary School in Birmingham, UK. This school, working in a relatively deprived urban context, introduced peer mediation in 1999 in response to difficult playtimes, but quickly moved to embracing it as offering much more than a reduction in aggressive play. Each year, mediation training is provided for key stage one children (six- to seven-year-olds) and they then provide a service for peers. As they go up through the school they receive top-up training and continue to offer a service. The peer mediators in this school also act as play leaders and friendship helpers, and other initiatives in the school also build on and reinforce peer mediation. The school has particular strengths in inclusion and home-school liaison, and these elements have contributed significantly to the success of the programme. The peer mediation coordinator in this school feels that outcomes of ECM have been met, and the children and their parents clearly value the opportunity of being a mediator. The mediators are both proud of their contribution and ambivalent about missing some of their playtimes.

Chapter 7 provides a second case study of a group of twenty four schools in Handsworth, Birmingham who introduced peer mediation as part of a community approach to reducing conflict. The project and its outcomes are outlined here.

Chapter 8 provides an overview of research into peer mediation to date, and suggests some flaws in that research. These flaws are explored within the two paradigms of interpretativist and positivist research. Much interpretative research into peer mediation is seen as lacking in rigour and as easily influenced by financial and professional interests, whereas positivist research into peer mediation is seen as often lacking in sensitivity and flexibility. Both can be poorly conceived and executed. A third area of concern stems from the ways in which research into peer mediation is conceptualized. It often relies on crude checklists of behaviours (such as levels of bullying and violence in school) and on psychometrics. These are heavily critiqued. My PhD research is reviewed as an example of a flawed experiment, and the implications of this flawed experiment for ongoing research into peer mediation are discussed. The book ends with recommendations for how research into peer mediation might be developed in the future.

As will be clear from the above, this book comes back to my research into peer mediation in three primary schools in Birmingham (Cremin, 2001) on a number of occasions. This research investigated whether peer mediation could have an impact on reducing bullying in these three schools. Measures chosen were frequency and nature of bullying, and students' feelings of self-esteem and empowerment. The three experimental schools (Schools One to Three) were chosen primarily because of their 'typicality' (Schofield, 1993), but also because, as a consortium, they had already expressed an interest in introducing peer mediation. The control school (school four) was chosen because it is within a mile radius of the experimental schools and has a similar socio-economic intake and ethnic mix. The schools in the research sample are urban elementary schools in the outer ring of Birmingham, UK.

A quasi-experimental research design, using both quantitative and qualitative analysis was used to address the main research questions. The independent variable was the implementation of a peer mediation service with all of the nine to ten-year-old students (N = 160) in three experimental schools. A professional development model was selected, which relied on class teachers training their own students without direct support in the classroom from the researcher. Thus, the seven class teachers from the three experimental schools were withdrawn from teaching for joint professional development on how to set up and support a peer mediation service. The professional development took place over two full days and two half days spread over six months. The teachers were trained in peer mediation methods, and circle time, and were given a peer mediation handbook (Stacey and Robinson, 1997).

The dependent variables were levels of bullying, attitudes towards bullying, and student levels of self-esteem and locus of control. Pretest and post-test measures were made using student questionnaires. Changes were analysed, using the Wilcoxon Matched-Pairs Signed Ranks Test, in terms of the numbers of children who experienced a reduction (in name calling or self-esteem, for example) or no change, between the first time of testing (the baseline) and the second time (when the peer mediation training was complete) between the second time and the third time (when the peer mediation service had been in place for six months) and between the first and the third time. Any change having a one-tailed probability value of 0.05 or less was taken here as significant. The locus of control (feelings of empowerment) questionnaire was taken from Nowicki and Strickland (1973), the self-esteem questionnaire was taken from Lawrence (1981), and the bullying questionnaire was taken from Tattum and Lane (1997). Supplementary qualitative data were collected through interviews to ascertain teacher perceptions of change in the attitudes, skills and behaviours of their students during the peer mediation training, and during the implementation of the peer mediation service. It will be noted that my attitude towards using a quasi-experiment to evaluate peer mediation evolved over the period of research, and the final chapter in particular contains a critique of some of the methods that I used. Some of the most illuminating data were collected from teacher interviews, and these rich and previously unpublished findings will be shared here in order to throw light on some of the themes that emerge throughout the book.

2 What is peer mediation?

Introduction

Mediation, as a form of dispute resolution, has come of age. It is as old as humankind, with roots in many cultures and world religions. It is practised widely in Asia and Africa as a traditional non-confrontational method of resolving conflict. Its current growth in popularity began in the 1970s in the US, and from there it has extended into Australia, Canada and many parts of Europe. It is extensively used within the legal profession, where it is part of a wider system of alternative dispute resolution (ADR) but its use has also extended into a wide range of other areas, including community mediation, victim-offender mediation, environmental mediation, peer mediation in schools, commercial mediation, family mediation, workplace mediation and intergroup conflict mediation. [It is the neutral, facilitative, voluntary and informal nature of mediation that make it distinct as a process of dispute resolution.] These are also the elements that give it the power to transform conflict and human relationships. This chapter will provide an overview of mediation in legal, community and education settings. It charts the growth of mediation, alternative dispute resolution (ADR) and restorative justice, and makes particular reference to transformative mediation. It goes on to provide perspectives on mediation from psychology and philosophy, some of which draw on traditional cultures from the global East and South, before focusing on peer support and peer mediation in schools. Finally, my research investigating the factors behind the success of peer mediation in 15 schools in Birmingham is reviewed, and conclusions are discussed.

What is mediation?

Despite (or perhaps because of) the speed of development in the field, definitions of the terms ADR and mediation remain uncrystalized, and, to an extent, contested. Although mediation has long been recognized by mediators, disputants, project workers, counsellors and academics from a variety of disciplines [as having social, practical and even transformative potential, there remains a surprising lack of consensus about the historical and theoretical underpinnings of mediation.] This is partly due to the diversity of its origins. Mediation has one foot in a tradition of community mediation and one foot in a legal tradition. How it is defined depends on the stance taken in various disciplines and stakeholder communities. American writers Baruch Bush and Folger give a loose definition of mediation as, 'an informal process in which a neutral third party with no power to impose a resolution helps the disputing parties to reach a mutually acceptable settlement' (2005: 8) but go on to suggest that there are four distinct 'stories' about mediation that influence how it is defined and practised: the satisfaction story; the social justice story; the transformation story and the oppression story. The first three are positive, the last one negative.

I definition

The satisfaction story holds that mediation is a powerful tool for satisfying human needs, enabling a quick, efficient and cost-effective resolution of disputes. It 'has led to more efficient use of private and public dispute resolution resources, which in turn means greater overall satisfaction for individual "consumers" of the justice system' (Baruch Bush and Folger, 2005). Proponents of this story include Fisher and Ury (1981). The social justice story holds that mediation can bring individuals together and build stronger communities. Mediators can work to limit exploitation, and create greater social justice that is more responsive to local need. Proponents of this story include Moore (1994). The transformation story holds that 'the unique promise of mediation lies in its capacity to transform the quality of conflict interaction itself, so that conflicts actually strengthen both the parties themselves and the society they are part of' (Baruch Bush and Folger, 2005, p.13). The oppression story holds that, despite good intentions, mediation has turned out to be a 'dangerous instrument for increasing power of the state over the individual and the power of the strong over the weak' (Ibid, p. 15). It goes on to articulate concern that the informality and consensuality of the process can lead to mediation being used as an inexpensive and expedient alternative to formal legal processes, denying disputants (usually the poor) proper access to the benefits of case law and human rights protection. Proponents of this story include Fiss (1984). The satisfaction and the oppression story tend to belong to a legal tradition of mediation, whereas the social justice and the transformation story tend to belong to a tradition of community mediation. These differences within legal and community traditions of mediation have led to divergences in practice. Mediation is practised in different ways, using different processes in different sectors.

negative

In commercial and employment mediation, for example, it is customary for all parties to meet briefly at the start of the process to share opening statements, after which the mediator facilitates a process of 'shuttle mediation' with the parties in separate rooms to protect commercial and industrial confidentiality. In community mediation, by contrast, the process usually starts with mediators visiting the disputing parties separately in their homes. The disputants can then meet face-to-face if and when they feel ready to do so. If they are unwilling to meet in the same room the process can continue through shuttle mediation. Family mediation has a tradition of working directly, face-to-face, with the disputants (unless there is a history of domestic violence) as does school-based peer mediation. Victim-offender mediation can be very powerful if parties are brought together, but the wishes of the victim are paramount, and a face-to-face meeting could only occur if all parties were willing and well prepared (Liebmann, 2000).

A variety of training and accreditation opportunities exist for mediators at all levels and in all sectors. Some sectors have a tradition of using volunteers (community mediation, peer mediation, some victim-offender mediation), others have sessionally paid workers (family mediation, medical mediation, some victim-offender mediation) and some mediators are salaried, or freelance professionals. Community mediation services tend to be free of charge, whereas mediation within legal settings can be on a par with solicitor's costs. Differences in remuneration and charging have as much to do with the philosophies of different traditions in mediation as they do with financial considerations (Liebmann, 2000). Grounded in notions of empowerment, empathic understanding and responsibility, community mediation services pass mediation skills and services on to as many members of the community as possible. Charitable or public-sector funding is often used to train volunteer mediators, who will then offer their services free of charge. Other mediation services concentrate on high quality service delivery for clients and prefer to use paid mediators in order to ensure consistency, reliability and accountability.

Mediation in legal settings

Within a legal framework, mediation has been defined as, 'a voluntary process where a neutral mediator attempts to help the disputing parties to reach an agreement that is acceptable to both sides and that will bring the dispute to an early conclusion without having to go to court' (Genn, 2000). Mediators working in legal settings are usually contrasted with arbitrators or judges, who, unlike mediators, have the authority to make judgements or to force the parties to reach an agreement or take a particular course of action. Table 2.1 provides a summary of what Genn (2000) sees as the advantages of mediation in legal settings, and confirms Baruch Bush and Folger's claim that mediation in legal settings is often defined in terms of the 'satisfaction story'.

Following pioneering work that was begun in Australia and America in the 1970s (for example Astor and Chinkin, 2001) a number of initiatives have institutionalized alternatives to litigation in the UK. One of the earliest adopters of mediation in the UK was ACAS, the Advisory, Arbitration and Conciliation Service, which provides mediation and arbitration for industrial disputes. ACAS, which has been functioning since 1975, is fully independent

Table 2.1 Genn's advantages of mediation

Flexibility	Mediation can be used for disputes over large or small sums of money, or for disputes that do not involve money, but are concerned with relationships or behaviour
Creative agreements	Mediation can achieve more creative solutions to disputes than would be possible through court proceedings. Decisions by judges are generally limited to providing financial compensation for things that have happened in the past; mediated agreements can include decisions about what might happen in the future
Repairing relationships	A skilled mediator can help to uncover misunderstandings and expose the real issues in dispute. In this way conflict can be reduced and it may, in the end, be possible to achieve reconciliation between private individuals or business people who are in a continuing relationship
Saving time and money	Mediation will often lead to quicker settlements than would be achieved through litigation procedures and, as a result of time-saving, can reduce legal and other costs
Reducing stress	Because of its informality and potential for time-saving, mediation offers dispute resolution that is less stressful for the parties than court litigation

Source: Genn (2000: 15–16)

and impartial, although it became a statutory body under the terms of the Employment Protection Act 1975 in January 1976. ACAS uses a comparatively directive form of mediation, and defines a mediator as someone who will:

> Assist parties involved in a dispute to find a mutually agreeable settlement. Usually the mediator will have powers to suggest a way forward and make formal recommendations. These recommendations are not binding, but parties are expected to seriously consider them as a basis for resolving the dispute.
>
> (ACAS, 2005: 10)

General reforms in civil justice procedure in the 1990s prompted a shift of attention from the 'trial' of issues in a formal setting to pre-trial activity (Glasser and Roberts, 1993). The Family Law Act (1996) introduced no-fault divorce proceedings, and required couples to consider whether mediation might be appropriate. The Act makes provision for legal aid for mediation in the same way as it does for legal representation. The Woolf (1996) reforms equipped judges with more powerful case-management tools, and the general trend is for the courts themselves to be more actively involved in pre-trial procedures. Put shortly, the focus has shifted from 'judgment' to 'settlement'. In a foreword to Hazel Genn's book, Lord Woolf (then Master of the Rolls) states that mediation offers, 'quick, cheap and constructive resolution of disputes'. He argues that it should be 'a primary aim of those involved in civil disputes to avoid going to court except as a last resort', and that 'mediation, which can take different forms, is probably the most effective method of resolving disputes without trial' (Genn, 2000: 9). He also acknowledges, however, that there is still a lot of ignorance about what it is, and how it can benefit parties involved in disputes.

One current example of mediation being used as an alternative to litigation is provided by the Central London County Court (CLCC) mediation scheme. Established as a pilot in 1996, the scheme has since become a permanent part of that court. It offers low-cost mediation in cases with a claim value above £5000 (the small claims limit). It was the first court mediation scheme of its kind in the UK and has served as a model for other court mediation schemes. The scheme's objective was to offer virtually cost-free court-annexed mediation to disputing parties at an early stage in litigation, involving a three-hour session with a trained mediator assisting parties to reach a settlement, with or without legal representation. The scheme's purpose was to promote swift dispute settlement and a reduction in legal costs through an informal process that parties might prefer to court proceedings. It was also thought that mediation would achieve savings in Legal Aid. The scheme has been entirely voluntary, and no party has been forced to use mediation. Reporting on her evaluation of the pilot phase of this project, Genn reports a 62 per cent settlement rate, and high levels of satisfaction amongst disputants (Genn, 1998). She proposes, however, that more needs to be done to educate the public and the legal profession about the benefits of ADR, following low demand for mediation (around 5 per cent of those who were offered it).

Liebmann (2000) also cites dissatisfaction with the legal system as a reason behind the growing use of mediation in the UK. She quotes from a survey carried out by the National Consumer Council (Taylor Nelson AGB, 1995) which found that about three-quarters of those who had experienced a serious dispute felt that the present legal system is too slow, complicated, old-fashioned, offputting and easy for those with sophisticated knowledge to manipulate. Asked about ways in which they would have preferred their conflict to be addressed, only 8 per cent favoured a full trial in court. Twenty three per cent opted for 'sitting round a table with an independent expert who makes the decision', and the majority, at 53 per cent, opted for 'sitting round a table with an independent expert who helps you to reach an agreement between yourselves' (Liebmann, 2000: 12). Clearly, increased use of mediation is linked with growing dissatisfaction with formality and inflexibility in the legal system. More recently, the Leggatt review of tribunals

(Leggatt, 2001) has led to a government White Paper (2004) that strongly advocates the use of 'proportionate dispute resolution' in a reformed administrative justice system. A Courts and Tribunals Bill aimed at delivering radical reforms in this area is expected to go through Parliament in the near future.

In the US, the use of mediation as a form of ADR continues to grow. The US Congress passed the Alternative Dispute Resolution Act in 1998. Under this Act all district courts now require litigants in civil cases to consider the use of ADR process at an appropriate stage in the litigation, and each district court has a responsibility to provide litigants in all civil cases with at least one ADR process. Also in the US, 'collaborative divorce' (Tesler, 2001) provides a sophisticated interdisciplinary dispute model that is gaining much attention. The model involves the use of a number of trained divorce coaches (mental health professionals) a neutral child specialist and neutral financial specialist. A disqualification agreement provides that if either party decides to litigate all of the professionals on the team are precluded from assisting in the litigation.

In Australia, structural pressures for reform have produced a rich range of ADR practice across the court, tribunal and ombudsmen systems at both the Commonwealth and State/Territory levels (Buck, 2005). Alternative dispute resolution is being mainstreamed in the federal civil justice system (Ruddock, 2004) and the government is committed to promoting and engaging in ADR in its role as a 'model litigant' (Buck 2005). Indeed, due to a proliferation of ADR methods and techniques the Australian National Alternative Dispute Resolution Advisory Council (NADRAC) has attempted to achieve greater consistency and confidence in ADR terminology by providing a glossary of terms (NADRAC, 1997, 2003). Spencer (2005) has noted that the growing adoption of ADR by the government in Australia is fast challenging the notion that such processes are indeed 'alternative'. Perhaps ironically, argument has raged within dispute resolution circles in Australia about the use of the word 'alternative'. Whilst litigators may see the word 'alternative' as being appropriate, many lawyers and non-litigators see the word as inaccurate. Over the years, some have suggested that the 'A' could refer to 'assisted' or 'appropriate' or 'additional' dispute resolution (Spencer, 2005: 17).

There has been an ambiguous response to ADR from the legal establishment. On the one hand it is seen as an appropriate response to structural pressures on justice systems. On the other, it threatens professional hierarchies and has also attracted powerful critiques suggesting that the position of vulnerable litigants is rarely made better where formal adjudication is replaced by informal justice (Abel 1982). It has been argued that the mediation process itself may undermine the authoritative pronouncement of judgments, which can be seen as performing the valuable function of stating and refurbishing key public values (Fiss 1984). The debate has acquired increased interest since the government's more recent interest in applying

ADR to core public law areas. To an extent, the increased pressures to deploy ADR conflicts with the development of a human rights culture following the UK's ingestion, in 1998, of the European Convention on Human Rights. Many feel that certain legal 'rights' ought to remain non-negotiable.

Acland (1995) has argued that it is important to know when mediation is appropriate and when it is not. Situations where it is not appropriate include when either party is unwilling or incapable of taking part or keeping to an agreement, when it is not really in one party's interests to settle, when there are threats or fear of violence, and when a dispute needs a public judgement. Liebmann (2000) has also warned of the dangers in an overenthusiastic use of mediation. It takes a good deal of mediator skill to balance power within a mediation where one party is more powerful than the other. Even with a very skilled mediator, disputants with little social capital might settle too quickly for less than they would be entitled to in law. There is evidence emerging that mediation is in danger of being used as 'cheap justice,' and that it might disguise corporate or public responsibility, and ignore human rights (Liebmann, 2000). She also notes that there are dangers that mediation might be a victim of its own success, with judges and other legal professionals mandating the mediation process. This could result in the cynical use of mediation, with one or both disputants going through the motions, rather than genuinely engaging with the process.

Baruch Bush and Folger (2005) refer to a variety of authors who have expressed concerns about the ways in which settlement-driven traditions of mediation threaten effective mediation practice. They locate dissatisfaction with mediation quite specifically with models which fail to empower and engage disputants in the resolution of their own conflict:

> In Sum, across the mediation field – whether in court, community, family or organisational settings – significant concerns have been raised about the prevailing, settlement-orientated approach to mediation practice ... the core of these concerns is that the focus on settlement has put at risk a set of values and benefits, private and public, that are even more important ... Those benefits are *self-determination* and *party interaction* or *engagement* – the core elements of the transformative model.
>
> (Baruch Bush and Folger, 2005: 95)

They make the point that the satisfaction model of mediation (which relies on satisfying needs and reducing unfairness) can make people temporarily better off, but problems are quickly replaced by new ones, and justice done is quickly undone. If mediation is to fulfil the promise of all that it can achieve, then transformative models of mediation will need to come to the fore.

Mediation and restorative justice

Mediation cannot be properly considered without a brief description of the philosophy and practices of restorative justice, which many see as an umbrella term encompassing mediation. Most restorative work involves processes of communication and aims for outcomes that empower victims, offenders and the wider communities to which they both belong. Mediation UK defines restorative justice as an approach which, 'centres around hearing what harm a crime has caused, and finding the best way to address that harm' (mediationuk.org, accessed August 2006). The key participants in restorative justice are communities, victims and offenders. The UK's criminal justice system is increasingly seeking to adopt restorative approaches to its work. The three main models of restorative justice practised within the UK are:

- victim-offender mediation
- family group conferencing
- restorative conferencing

Victim-offender mediation is a form of mediation that allows an offender to make some form of reparation to his or her victim. The victim is also given space to ask any questions about the offence (typically – 'Why me? Will it happen again?') and to communicate to the offender the extent of the harm that has been done. Some cases involve a face-to-face meeting, although more often the parties choose shuttle mediation.

Family group conferencing is used in a variety of contexts, not just in the context of restorative justice, and provides a forum for a group of people (sometimes including the victim of a crime) to provide support for an individual, usually a young person, who needs to make an important life decision. Restorative conferencing is a more structured process, where a conference facilitator, who often works from a standard script, asks a set of (mainly open) questions in a certain order, enabling all the participants to speak. Participants include the young people in question, their immediate caregivers and any friends, extended family or professionals who may be able to play a supportive role, the victim(s) of the offence(s) (if they wish to attend) and supporters of the victim. This script is designed to bring about group interaction and communication likely to achieve a number of objectives related to the health and wellbeing of the victim and the offender, and to the reduction in crime and antisocial behaviour.

The Home Office in the UK is supportive of restorative justice as an approach to reducing crime. It notes, 'where "traditional justice" is about punishing offenders for committing offences against the state, restorative justice is about offenders making amends directly to the people or organisations they have harmed' (www.homeoffice.gov.uk, accessed August 2006). It supports restorative justice because it gives victims a greater voice in the criminal justice system, allowing them to receive an explanation and more meaningful reparation from offenders, and because it makes offenders accountable by allowing them to take responsibility for their actions. It also builds community confidence that offenders are making amends for their wrongdoing. Pilot studies cited by the Home Office indicate that restorative justice approaches can reduce post-traumatic stress disorder in victims, and in some cases motivate offenders to turn away from a life of crime. They make the point that restorative justice is not a soft option, as many offenders find it extremely difficult to face up to the impact of their crimes. Restorative Justice has been applied in educational settings for a number of years internationally. Much of this work has been carried out in the US, Canada and Australia (Braithwaite, 2001; McCold, 2003; Morrison, 2003).

Mediation in community settings

Mediation in community settings tends to be facilitative and non-directive, and focuses more on the repair and maintenance of relationships than on quasi-legal processes. Mediation UK, the main umbrella organization for mediation in Britain, defines mediation as, 'a well established process for resolving disagreements in which an impartial third party (the mediator) helps people in dispute to find a mutually acceptable resolution' (http://mediationuk.org.uk) The key elements of neutrality, facilitation, informality and cooperation are clear here, as is the importance of the mediator's lack of power over the disputants, other than in assisting them to keep within the agreed boundaries of the mediation process. Drawing on her own work, and that of Cornelius and Faire (1989), Liebmann (2000: 12–13) lists a set of values and ideas which are implicit in community mediation work. These are:

- listening to others, for feelings as well as facts;
- cooperation with others, valuing their contributions;
- looking for common ground rather than differences;
- affirmation of self and others as a necessary basis for resolving conflict;
- speaking for oneself rather than accusing others;
- separating the problem from the people;
- trying to understand other people's point of view;
- using a creative problem-solving approach to work on conflicts;
- looking at what people want for the future rather than allocating blame for the past;
- looking at all the options before selecting one to try;

- looking for a 'win-win' solution, where everyone's interests are satisfied, rather than the adversarial 'win-lose' approach where one person wins and the other person loses.

It is clear from the above list that community mediation shares some values and practices with legal traditions of mediation, but that it also shares values and practices with certain forms of counselling, as well as with facilitative management techniques, and with traditional forms of community-led dispute resolution from different parts of the world. It is the values of facilitation, active listening, empathy, cooperation and empowerment that unite community mediation services and practitioners more than any set of procedures or models of practice.

Liebmann lists the benefits of these forms of mediation (Liebmann, 2000: 11). She recognizes that a key benefit is that it encourages disputants to focus on the problem rather than on each other. Mediators help disputants to identify common ground and look for the way forward. It gives both parties a chance to tell their side of the story, focusing on the harm done, and to feel heard by the other party. People are more likely to change their actions if they hear how their behaviour is affecting the other person and if they have been involved in reaching a solution – rather than being subjected to an imposed solution. Because disputants play a central role in deciding the outcomes of their dispute, mediation is able to support them to focus on their individual needs, and on the complex and unique nature of their dispute. Mediation's flexibility enables a dispute to be looked at in the round and enables its many strands to be examined, including those that have no basis in law. In these ways, compared with more formal and traditional processes of dispute resolution, community mediation de-emphasizes jurisdiction and places its emphasis on psycho-social processes.

The process of mediation that is currently used in the UK in community projects came from the US in the 1980s. In the 1970s, the administration of President Jimmy Carter encouraged the creation of the first Neighbourhood Justice Centres. The goal of these centres, often known as 'community mediation programmes', was to provide an alternative to court proceedings where citizens could meet to resolve their disputes. Some of the most active of these centres were in New York, Los Angeles, and Philadelphia. In the typical community mediation programme, a cross-section of neighbourhood volunteers was trained to mediate the disputes that arose in their community, including disputes between neighbours, family members, tenants and landlords/landladies, consumers and salespeople, friends and small businesses. Some disputes were referred directly to the centre by local residents; others came through an affiliation with local courthouses and social service agencies. The success of these early programmes was impressive (Cohen, 1995). They thrived in a post-1960s climate that demanded non-violent, localized responses to conflict. Exponents in the field (see for example Beer et al., 1987) were often motivated by strong personal convictions, and sought to enskill and empower citizens to resolve their own disputes in ways that would strengthen communities, and enable individuals to live more satisfying lives (Cremin, 2001).

For many, a philosophy of non-violence underpins mediation. This philosophy can be traced to different world religions. In the US and the UK, the Religious Society of Friends (Quakers) have played an important role in supporting the growth of community mediation. The Quaker tradition of non-violence goes back to 1661 when George Fox, the founder member, testified to Charles the Second that he would not take up weapons against any man. This pacifism has continued to the present day, with a long tradition of informal Quaker mediation in many of the trouble spots of the world. John McConnell and Adam Curle (a Quaker who has held professorships at Exeter, Ghana, Harvard and Bradford) are two such mediators who have written about their work and beliefs (Curle, 1981; McConnell, 1992).

Community mediation continues to thrive in both the US and the UK. Mediation UK notes that 40,000 people were involved in community mediation between 2004 and 2005 (http://www.mediationuk.org.uk) and that over 200 community mediation services now deal with conflicts between neighbours in the UK. Many of these community mediation services also offer training for students and teachers in schools as part of a preventative approach to dealing with conflict in the community. One example of such a community mediation service is Cardiff Mediation Service. Cardiff Mediation is a city-wide community mediation service which has been fully operational since 1996. Since 1999 it has come under the umbrella of Mediation Wales, which also supports community mediation in five other areas of Wales. Cardiff Mediation primarily takes referrals from housing, statutory and voluntary agencies on behalf of disputing neighbours, but disputants can also self refer. The service is independently constituted as a charity, and has two full-time members of staff (a coordinator and a case-manager) who support 30 to 40 volunteer mediators (Waddington, 2000). Another example of a community mediation service is Lincolnshire Mediation. The following case study is taken from their Web site (http://www.lfms.org.uk/mediation_case_studies. html, accessed Jan 2007):

> Mr and Mrs S and Mr and Mrs B had been neighbours for 3 years and from the time they met they had not 'seen eye to eye'. This had started after an argument between their children, had worsened after damage had been noticed to one of the party's cars while it was parked in the street, and blocking in on the shared driveway had also occurred. Name calling and 'watching' had also been cited as problems and the police and housing officer had been called out on

many occasions to see both parties. Solicitors' letters had also been exchanged and the problems were escalating...

Both parties wanted a cessation of hostilities even though they had no idea how a solution might emerge and they wanted nothing to do with the other. To their credit, both parties agreed to try mediation even though this meant potentially having to meet together. Separate information-gathering meetings were organised with each couple during which mediators at LM were able to hear the extent of the disagreement and explain to the clients how mediation works. Both couples said they wanted to resolve their situation and agreed to meet together in the safe physical and emotional space offered at Lincolnshire Mediation.

A subsequent meeting was arranged for all parties where the couples and the mediators met together. The ground rules of mediation were explained and each couple had the chance to explain their feelings about the situation and then they were able to respond to each other. At times the exchanges were very heated but with LM mediators holding the space for the meeting and helping the parties to work within their ground-rules. Frustrations were evident at different times when Mr S left the room and Mrs B did likewise having become extremely upset. After a break the situation gradually became calmer and the mediators were able to help the couples begin to look towards the future and at what they would like to happen. Both couples came up with very similar ideas and some tentative conversation began. Mrs B said 'how did we get from there to here?' Mrs S said 'we may not end up being close friends but we should now be able to talk with each other if anything arises in the future'. With the help of the mediators, an agreement was put together and signed by all the parties.

Feedback from the police indicates that since this successful mediated outcome, the dispute is at an end and no further police time has been used on it.

Much current community mediation practice in the UK is grounded in Baruch Bush and Folger's 'transformative view' of mediation. They argue that this transformative potential is far more valuable than mediation's other benefits, important though these are, as transformative models are essentially educative and go beyond the resolution of individual conflicts. This is not to say that transformative mediation aims to transform people's character, or redistribute resources or power, or to offer advice advocacy or counselling. Transformative mediation aims merely to enable 'dynamic shifts' from one mode of experiencing self and others to a different mode. Long-term benefits can include what some have called 'upstream effects' (Hallberlin, 2001) that carry over into future situations. Baruch Bush and Folger (2005) claim that public benefits of transformative mediation advance the goals of society as a whole, and that these benefits are often overlooked, as most discussions of the public benefit of mediation focus on its value in saving public resources, especially court costs.

Antes et al. (2001) carried out a study of the changes that occurred as a result of the REDRESS programme, which uses transformative mediation in the US Postal Service. The following outcomes were noted as part of this study (Antes et al., 2001: 69)

- participants move from strong emotion to calm, from defensiveness to openness, and from speaking about or at the other party to interacting with them;
- participants interact more confidently as the mediation progresses;
- interactions that are negative and difficult often lead to discussions that are positive and productive;
- participants establish or re-establish personal connections with each other;
- participants gain new understandings during the mediation about the other party and their actions, about themselves and their own actions and about the situation;
- discussion of a specific incident often leads participants to talk about larger issues that are significant to their relationships and the workplace.

These outcomes could be seen as cultural shifts within the workplace, and show how transformational mediation can have impacts that go beyond the resolution of individual disputes. It is these key benefits which flag up the potential of mediation in school settings. This will be further explored later in this chapter.

The next section of this chapter will review some perspectives on conflict and mediation from psychology and philosophy. This will create a theoretical grounding for the review of peer mediation in schools contexts that will follow.

Perspectives on mediation from psychology

A branch of psychology that can usefully be applied to the study of conflict and mediation is social psychology. In the early days of social psychology figures such as Darwin, Marx and Freud dominated the intellectual atmosphere, emphasizing the competitive and destructive aspects of conflict and neglecting the more positive and cooperative models of conflict resolution

(Deutsch and Coleman, 2000). In the 1930s, Lewin's field theory created a new vocabulary for thinking about the positive as well as the negative aspects of conflict, cooperation and competition. Employing his analysis of force fields, Lewin presented a theoretical discussion of three basic types of psychological conflict: approach-approach, avoidance-avoidance, and approach-avoidance (Lewin, 1935). Von Neumann and Morgenstern's game theory in the 1950s developed these ideas further, and a theory of cooperation and competition was eventually formalized by Deutsch (1949, 1973) and elaborated by Johnson and Johnson (1989). The theory has two basic ideas. One relates to the type of interdependence amongst goals of people in a given situation. The other pertains to the type of action taken by the people involved:

> In brief, the theory equates a constructive process of conflict resolution with an effective cooperative problem-solving process, in which the conflict is the mutual problem to be resolved cooperatively. It also equates a destructive process of conflict resolution with a competitive process, in which the conflicting parties are involved in a competition or struggle to determine who wins and who loses; often the outcome of the struggle is loss for both parties.
>
> (Deutsch, 2000: 30)

Thus, conflict is neither good nor bad, neither constructive nor destructive; outcomes depend on the ways in which conflict is handled. Third parties (mediators) can intervene in a dispute in order to maximize the chances of a constructive outcome, and disputants can be taught ways of avoiding the violent escalation of disputes. These theories of conflict resolution have played an important role in shaping the ways in which mediation has grown over the past few decades.

Ausburger (1992) an anthropologist and social psychologist, writes about the impact of culture on attitudes towards conflict and mediation. He argues that conflict is often handled badly in modern Western individualistic cultures, with negative psychological consequences for individuals and society at large. The first of these negative consequences comes from the repression of shame:

> Individualistic societies repress shame experience, inhibit its resolution, and arrest development at the earliest stage with guilt being over-developed as a cover and as a major psychic administrator of internal control. When shame is felt, it is in primitive and infantile rage and self-immolation, as the face burns. In more collective

cultures, the maturation of both shame and guilt may be fostered, and the internal controls function conjointly and cooperatively.

(Ausburger, 1992: 82)

In traditional collectivist cultures of the global East and South, honour and shame are powerful reciprocal forces that serve to unite groups, police the boundaries, define who is included and excluded, and enforce conformity. Mediation is assumed as a communal necessity. Modern Western societies rely instead on law as an abstract system of codified rules, collected cases, and established precedents. As Ausburger (1992: 191) points out, in human relational terms 'this is not the most effective or satisfactory pattern.' Mediation can be used to reinstate some of these lost social psychological approaches.

Another of the negative psychological consequences of the ways in which conflict is handled in individualistic cultures stems from an absence of celebration. Ausburger (1992: 240) notes that, 'Celebration, the missing step in much conflict, is the crucial element that confirms the learnings that have resulted from the preceding steps.' This is lacking in many urban Western social contexts, including schools, where busy teachers, teaching assistants and heads move on too quickly once a conflict has been resolved through a child's generosity, ability to forgive, or sheer pragmatism. These valuable opportunities for affirmation, recognition and reinforcement are often lost, with detrimental effects on social learning.

Ausburger (1992: 243) lists a number of 'conflict myths' that have arisen in Western individualistic cultures and are damaging to psychological health. They also inhibit the use of mediation. Confession, he contends, is not ventilation, dissipation, justification, or flagellation; it is the authentic recognition of responsibility for one's acts and their consequences. Contrition is not punitive, self-condemnation, obsessive remorse, manipulative kowtowing, or expiatory grovelling; it is appropriate sorrow for one's wrong behaviour. Restitution is not a repayment to avoid retaliation (anxiety) or return of equivalent value to earn acceptance (shame); it is the re-establishing of mutual justice (resolving guilt and responsibility). Reconciliation is not a vertical restoration of unjust structures that may have been part of the process of the injury; it is a joint process of releasing the past with its pain, restructuring the present with new reciprocal respect and acceptance, and reopening the future to new risks and spontaneity. Forgiveness is not an arbitrary, free act of pardon given out of the unilateral generosity of the forgiver; it is an interpersonal transaction between two parties.

A newly conceived notion of conflict resolution and mediation for the twenty-first century would draw on global and intercultural perspectives on conflict and justice. Traditional cultures see conflict as a communal concern; the group has ownership of the conflict and context. Western urban cultures, by contrast, see conflict as an individual concern, often focusing on personal issues or private ownership. People in Western urban cultures are much more likely to use a confrontational, direct-address, one-to-one negotiating style, or at least believe that that is the final way to resolve differences. People in traditional cultures are more likely to possess a non-confrontational, indirect, triangular resolution style. Traditional cultures value harmony, solidarity, interdependence, honour, and the maintaining of face, hierarchy and status differentials, whereas urban Western cultures value individualism, autonomy, independence, self-reliance, self-esteem, quality, and egalitarianism (Ausburger, 1992: 32).

Baruch Bush and Folger's (2005) transformative mediation sets itself against the Western urban ideology of individualism. Underlying the ideology of transformative mediation is the notion that there is, 'an *inherent supply* of the capacity for strength and connection in human beings, rather than an inherent deficit' (Baruch Bush and Folger, 2005: 250) so that a codified system of law is not necessary for conflict to move in a productive rather than destructive direction. Mediation has much to offer in restoring psychological health and wellbeing in situations of conflict.

Another branch of psychology that informs the study of mediation is humanistic psychology. Early models of community mediation were developed in the US in therapeutic settings. They took their lead from Rogerian humanistic counselling, in which the client remains in charge of the process throughout, and the therapist shows empathy, unconditional positive regard and genuineness towards the client (Rogers, 1951). Core aims of humanistic counselling include the need to restore the self-esteem of the client, and to encourage a more internal locus of control. Mediation can be seen as a means of bringing these benefits to interpersonal disputes, although care should be taken not to confuse mediation with counselling or therapy, both of which require training and supervision which are not always available or desirable for mediators (Cremin, 2001).

Humanistic psychology is a reaction against the mechanistic theories of behaviourism and psychoanalysis. Whereas behaviourism emphasizes conditioned learning, and psychoanalysis emphasizes the effect of early experiences stored in the unconscious, humanistic psychology implies that human beings are complex and capable of exercising choice, rather than being victims of past experience. Humanistic psychology has, as a guiding principle, that the individual possesses a natural ability to develop to his or her full potential, a process that Maslow called 'self-actualisation', and in this it represents an optimistic rather than a pathological view of human nature.

This belief in the ability of human beings to resolve difficulties with support from an empathic and caring third party is fundamental to the theoretical underpinning of mediation, particularly transformative mediation as described above. Baruch Bush and Folger (2005) speak of destructive, alienating and demonizing approaches to conflict as a downwards spiral in which disputants feel weak and self-absorbed. They suggest that constructive, connecting and humanizing approaches to conflict can lead to disputants feeling strong and responsive to the perspective of others and that this upwards spiral is enabled through the key elements of empowerment and recognition. Thus transformative mediation can be seen as a powerful psycho-social tool in bringing about healthier and more effective conflict resolution.

Perspectives on mediation from philosophy

If humanism can be seen in the psychological roots of mediation, it can also be seen in its philosophical roots. Mediation is connected to the concept of humanism but also, paradoxically, to its decline in the twentieth century. Mediation is grounded in the ability of human beings to find solutions to their own problems, without recourse to external authority, or to religious ideas about right and wrong. In this respect it is the ultimate human-centred mode of conflict resolution, based on an optimistic view of human nature. This view of 'man' was at its strongest in the nineteenth century, and found expression in Locke, Comte, Nietzsche and Matthew Arnold, the innovative headteacher of Rugby School.

The term 'humanism' is of German coinage, and was first used in the Middle Ages to describe a humanities curriculum based on ancient Greek and Latin literature and history. In the fifteenth century it became associated with Renaissance ideas of learning, and in the nineteenth century the twin pillars of classics and competitive games supported the curriculum in Matthew Arnold's Rugby School. For Arnold, the 'central truly human point of view', though evidently modern and European, stood for something essential, above and beyond the accidents of historical or national difference (Davies, 1997).

The nineteenth century saw humanism take a new turn when it was used to describe a form of secular religion. Nietzsche's famous affirmation that 'God is dead' built on a systematic account of a 'religion of humanity' supplied by the positivist Augustus Comte. The promise of the Enlightenment in the eighteenth century, grounded in reason, science, and respect for humanity, continued into the nineteenth century through humanism. A God-shaped hole in the nineteenth-century psyche was filled with the promise of man, and all that he was set to achieve through science, innovation and economic growth.

The twentieth century, however, saw a gradual erosion of the optimism of the nineteenth century. Marx, Freud, and Darwin unsettled the human subject from his previously secure place at the centre of the universe, and revealed his unwitting dependence on laws and structures outside of his control and sometimes beyond his knowledge. The modern world had enabled industrial capitalism and huge scientific advances, but it had also enabled Auschwitz, the threat of nuclear war, the horrors of Nazism and Stalinism, neocolonialism, Eurocentrism, racism, global warming and Third World hunger. If the nineteenth century had witnessed the death of God, the twentieth century could be seen as witnessing the death of man, at least in his white, male, Western, educated, heterosexual incarnation. The 'postmodern turn' at the end of the twentieth century left very little ground for the human subject to stand upon. To quote Foucault, 'As the archaeology of our thought easily shows, man is an invention of recent date. And one perhaps nearing its end' (Foucault, 1970: 386–7). Humanism, truth, meaning, even language itself, were considerably undermined. This had a profound effect on the ways in which conflict and justice were perceived. Modern and postmodern thought were marked by experimentation, and by the realization that knowledge and justice are not absolute.

For Matthew Arnold, it was self-evident that the essence of man was grounded in white, European, male perspectives, but once human reason began to be historicized in the twentieth century, the notion that the philosopher could by means of reason discover universal truths and value became more difficult to sustain (Matthews, 1996). Perhaps the earliest significant twentieth-century thinker to question the basis of humanism was Jean-Paul Sartre. For Sartre, there is no abstract humanity working towards the fulfilment of its own essential nature. In *L'Etre et le Néant* (*Being and Nothingness*), he states, 'I *am* as the Other sees me' (Sartre, 1943: 222) there is no essential inner life. The self is what is constructed through actions in the world. Bad faith (*mauvaise foi*) refers to the cultivated illusion by which we seek to conceal from ourselves the uncomfortable ambiguity of our position – that we can and must choose, without recourse to any external authority. 'To be free agents, for Sartre, is at once to acknowledge the constraints of our situation – of our place in space and time, of our physical characteristics, of our individual past, and of the point in history in which we exist – and to transcend those constraints in our actions' (Sartre 1943: 68). The work of Sartre is inextricably linked with the work of Simone de Beauvoir (they were partners living in Paris at the same time). Her work marked the beginnings of the feminist perspectives on philosophy that have done so much to undermine philosophy's traditional masculinist assumptions.

Perhaps the most sustained and fatal attack on humanism can be found in the writings of the structuralists. Structuralism appeared in the second half of the twentieth century, when it became one of the most popular ways of approaching language, culture and society. Ferdinand de Saussure began to write about structuralism through his work on linguistics, although the term 'structuralism' itself appeared in relation to French anthropologist Claude Lévi-Strauss' works, and gave rise, in France, to the 'structuralist movement', which gathered thinkers such as Lacan, Foucault and Althusser. As Matthews points out, 'What was distinctive about Saussure's approach to language was his insistence on studying, not the historical processes of change in particular languages, but the underlying structures which are common to language as such' (Matthews, 1996: 135). He goes on, 'the adoption of a structuralist approach, whether in linguistics or in anthropology ... carries with it important philosophical implications. It undermines the view of language (and so of thought) as a transparent representation of an objective reality: it is not the nature of the world which determines the concepts which we can have of it, but the reverse' (Matthews, 1996: 138). This undermines all metaphysical doctrines of the possibility of absolute knowledge. Davies puts it differently:

> In this way, structuralism kicks away the twin pillars of humanism: the sovereignty of rational consciousness, and the authenticity of individual speech. I do not think, I am thought. You do not speak, you are spoken. Thought and speech, which for the humanist have been the central substance of identity, are located elsewhere, and the self is a vacancy.
>
> (Davies, 1997:61)

Foucault (1977) applied these ideas to concepts of justice and punishment in his book *Discipline and Punish: the Birth of the Prison*. He proposed that the power to control and punish has been fragmented, and that powerful 'discourses' rise, swell, flow and ebb throughout all kinds of social interaction. The discourses themselves have no particular origin in history, there are no perpetrators, no victims, no 'grand narratives' that unify or systematize ways of thinking. These discourses 'just are' and continue to evolve and develop in their own unpredictable way. The human agent can choose how to respond to these discourses but cannot escape their effects. For example, a black male of African origin in a school cannot help but be affected by discourses concerning underachievement and delinquency in Black African-Caribbean males. He can choose to conform to the stereotype, he can do the opposite, but he cannot escape the effects of the discourse itself. Even if his teachers are using all kinds of approaches to ensure that they do not unwittingly discriminate, they are also part of shaping and continuing the discourse. For Foucault, there is no clear site of struggle; the human subject is not free to use his or her agency to bring about emancipation for him or herself or for others. These discourses gain impetus from complexity and fragmentation, and their effect on the human psyche and on issues of justice and conflict are hard to pin down:

> Throughout the penal procedure and the implementation of the sentence there swarms a whole series of subsidiary authorities. Small scale legal systems and parallel judges have multiplied around the

> principle judgement: psychiatric or psychological experts, magis-
> trates concerned with the implementation of the sentence, educa-
> tionalists, members of the prison service, all fragment the legal power
> to punish . . .
>
> (Foucault, 1977: 21)

The implications of structuralism for mediation are clear. Traditional jurisdiction has relied on the idea of a unified narrative, legitimized by history and grounded in the authority of the wise and the good of each generation. Justice for all, at least in theory, has been the aspiration of the legal profession. But in a social world shaped by powerful discourses beyond the control of individuals or groups, characterized by fragmentation and complexity, and quite literally 'lost for words', truth and justice are relative concepts: it depends on where you are standing and who you are. Mediation offers locally based solutions to particular disputes. It lays no claim to objective truth or justice; it merely aims to facilitate a process in which disputants can find a solution that is 'good enough' within their own terms of reference. Paradoxically, as Baruch Bush and Folger (2005) have pointed out, this can lead to a transformation in the way in which conflict is perceived, but this is not to suggest that mediation is grounded in any essentialist view of human nature.

Two thinkers who have taken opposite stances to these Foucauldian ideas are the German, Habermas, and the Frenchman, Derrida. Whilst Habermas worked to rescue the modernist quest for emancipation through language, non-dominating interpersonal relations and a broader notion of reason, Derrida claimed that language and power are too closely entangled for any such rescue attempt to be successful. Habermas aimed to integrate the normative aspects of philosophical reflection with the explanatory achievements of the social sciences. He felt that theory and practice could be linked through rational insights, empowering human subjects to change their oppressive circumstances and satisfy their needs.

Habermas's epistemology is grounded in the discourse that transpires in 'ideal speech situations'. These have strong links with the mediation process. When all of the ordinary constraints on the free exchange of ideas (such as differences in status, power, authority, and ethos) are lifted, Habermas believed that discourse between individuals would allow them to reach a consensus about truth and the validity of norms. Thus, truth does not reside 'out there', but instead resides within the community. The 'ideal speech situation' requires 'fair play' in dialogue. All participants must have equal opportunity to participate. They must have the right to assert, defend or question any factual or normative claim, and they must be motivated solely by the desire to reach a consensus. The extent to which a speech situation is 'ideal' depends on a variety of other antecedents ranging from considerations of cultural traditions to the distribution of material resources. It also depends on the 'communicative competence' of the participants, the second of Habermas's key concepts for rhetoric. This competence centres on the aspect of language that allows us to differentiate between three domains of reference: the subjective, the inter-subjective, and the objective. Links between Habermas's ideal speech situations and the mediation process are strong. Both rely on the establishment of firm ground rules, and on the willingness of both parties to engage in open, honest dialogue, with the aim or reaching consensus.

Habermas has been widely criticized as being out of step with the considerations of a postmodern world. For example, although he recognizes the plurality of modern society, he nevertheless sees the ideal speech situation as ultimately requiring a consensus for epistemic justification. Habermas and Derrida engaged in somewhat acrimonious disputes, beginning in the 1980s and culminating in a refusal to engage in extended debate until quite recently. One important way in which Derrida felt that traditional philosophy in general, and Habermas's philosophy in particular, had gone astray is that it is too 'logocentric'. Matthews (1996: 168–9) suggests that, for Derrida

> What remains of philosophy will be, not the construction of such general theories, but the simple activity of fundamental questioning as such. And this fundamental questioning will clearly not, given the rejection of 'logocentrism', take the form of logical assessment of arguments.

Derrida has moral and political objections to Western ethnocentrism.

> His 'deconstruction' of the philosophical tradition is meant to expose the tension between surface attachment to Enlightenment ideals of universal humanity and rationality and the underlying sense that these ideals in fact inhere only in the particular values of a particular historical culture, that of western Europe and the other parts of the world which have been influenced by Europe.
> (Matthews, 1996:176)

Derrida was already extremely ill by the time he and Habermas finally resumed their contact with each other. This was in an interview with Borradori, three months after 9/11. Sadly, they were unable to complete the process of revisiting their disagreements *vis-à-vis* the other, but their views were surprisingly similar, and show perhaps certain pragmatism in these challenging times for global peace and security. Habermas refers to 'intangibility' that lends a new quality to the terrorism of groups like al-Qaeda, and remarks that these terrorists 'allow their religious motives of a fundamentalist kind to be known, though they do not pursue a program that goes beyond the engineering of destruction and insecurity' (Borradori, 2003: 4). He criticizes the Bush administration for, 'continuing, more or less undisturbed, the self-centred course of a callous superpower' (Borradori, 2003: 5) and for fighting against the appointment of an international criminal court, relying instead on military tribunals of its own. He goes on, 'The world has grown too complex for this barely concealed unilateralism. Even if Europe does not rouse itself to play the civilizing role, as it should, the emerging power of China and the waning power of Russia do not fit into the *pax Americana* model so simply' (Borradori, 2003: 6).

Likewise, Derrida remarks on the nihilism of Bin Laden's discourse, and makes the point that if he had to choose between the two camps he would, 'take the side of the camp that, in principle, by right of law, leaves a perspective open to perfectibility in the name of the "political," democracy, international law, international institutions, and so on' (Borradori, 2003: 25). He goes on:

> Even if this 'in the name of' is still merely an assertion and a purely verbal commitment, even in its most cynical mode, such an assertion still lets resonate within it an invincible promise. I don't hear any such promise coming from 'Bin Laden,' at least not one for *this world*.
> (Borradori, 2003: 27)

Third-party intervention through international law and organizations such as the United Nations is seen by both Habermas and Derrida as being the response to global terrorism that shows 'the best possible fit', despite its imperfections. This new pragmatism fits more closely with an American tradition of philosophy. Working from within an Anglo-American philosophical tradition, Rorty argues that the age of what he calls 'Philosophy with a capital P' (Rorty, 1979) is now past and discredited because of the work of such thinkers as William James, Dewey, Heidegger and Wittgenstein. 'What must replace "Philosophy," Rorty argues, is "philosophy," which will simply be a part, along with literature and art, of the "conversation of mankind", concerned to produce, not "truth", but images of how we might live our lives' (Matthews, 1996: 174). Similarly, Lyotard has argued that what postmodern society needs are rather local initiatives, on a small scale, informed by local traditions and seeking reform of concrete injustices.

Third-party intervention, small-scale responses to concrete injustices, attempts to find solutions that do not make claims to objective or universal truth, pluralism, and local action; all of these are linked to the theory and practice of mediation. Mediation is not always suitable or appropriate, but it is a proportionate and apt response to many conflicts that arise in these complex and fragmented times. Quoting Heidegger, Derrida suggests that a humanism that depends on a certain conception of the 'essence of man' is inimical to true humanity. 'We become truly human, in fact, by "mediating" and "caring", by recognising ourselves primarily in our relation to "the truth of Being", in harmony with Being as a whole' (Matthews, 1996: 175).

Peer support

Peer mediation is a form of peer support. Peer support in schools takes a number of different forms, including peer-led pastoral care systems, befriending, mentoring and, of course, peer mediation (Sharp, 2001). Peer tutoring (Topping, 1996) and peer counselling (Cowie and Sharp, 1996; McNamara, 1996; Webb and Kaye, 1996) are perhaps the best-known forms of peer support. Huddleston and Kerr (2006) describe peer counselling at Frederick Gough school, Bottesford. Year nine students apply and are selected following a school assembly. They are given parental support, and then receive 10 one-and-a-half hour sessions of training after school from an outside agency. The training covers such areas as issues of confidentiality, and what can and can't be discussed with fellow students. They advertise their service and then begin to offer appointments at lunchtimes. During the sessions notes are kept, which are then locked away for safekeeping. The role of the member of staff supporting the service is key – not least to provide support mechanisms for the peer counsellors themselves, and to deal with child protection issues, should they arise. Peer mediation will now be explored in more depth.

Peer mediation

In the 1980s, in the US, a range of social, political and pedagogical influences combined to create ideal conditions for the growth of peer mediation (Cohen, 1995). Social problems were causing numerous problems for schools. Despite educators' best efforts, student conflicts and violence were increasing, and as a result schools were more willing than usual to look outside the educational establishment for assistance. Peer mediation was seen as an additional tool that did nothing to detract from existing structures of conflict management in school. It was seen as a practicable and measurable process (in contrast to peace education that was seen as vague and politically charged) and it had the added advantage of being visible and media friendly. Peer education programmes generally had captured the interest of educators, and the growth in legal and community mediation highlighted above led to an increased understanding of alternative dispute resolution amongst the general public. In 1984 a small group of community mediators and educators formed the National Association for Mediation in Education. At that time, only a handful of peer mediation programmes existed. Currently there are many thousands located in schools in every state of the US.

Throughout the late 1980s, 1990s and into the new century the use of peer mediation has extended to many different parts of the world. Its use is widespread in Canada (Bickmore, 2001), Australia and New Zealand (Cameron and Dupuis, 1991; McMahon, 1997) and educational practices that involve peer mediation are growing more common in Europe (ENCORE, 1997). In the UK, the Kingston Friends Workshop Group was amongst the first to adapt American peer mediation training materials for British students (Kingston Friends Working Group, 1985). In 1989 Walker's paper on violence and conflict resolution in schools, commissioned by the European Union, included information about peer mediation and led to the formation of the European Network of Conflict Resolution in Education, which is supported by British Quakers and continues to meet annually for a conference. There has been a particular interest in conflict resolution training and peer mediation in Northern Ireland as part of the Education for Mutual Understanding (EMU) curriculum (Tyrrell and Farrell, 1995).

In the early 1990s, the climate in schools in the UK was receptive to peer mediation, as the climate in American schools had been 10 years earlier. There were other initiatives in education at that time based on similar humanistic, active learning, student-centred value systems. A greater emphasis on group-work, cooperative games and problem solving aimed to improve young people's ability to cooperate, for example Masheder (1986); Leimdorfer (1990); Bennett and Dunne (1992); Horbury and Pears (1994). Classroom practice encouraging individualized and autonomous learning tried to give young people a more internal locus of control, for example Waterhouse (1983); Brandes and Gintis (1990); Roberts (1994); Maines and Robinson (1994). A focus on speaking and listening skills, for example Barnes (1984); National Curriculum Council (1989); Bliss and Tetley (1993) and Powell and Makin (1994), aimed to improve students' ability to communicate. A growing awareness of the importance of high self-esteem, for example Maines and Robinson (1988) and White (1991), meant that many teachers were working to establish positive 'affirming' relationships with young people. Above all, what these initiatives stressed is the importance of student empowerment and social and affective skills for life. Some schools, which had begun the process of empowering students to take more responsibility for the quality of life in school, found that peer mediation was a natural next step to take. This is not to underplay the equally powerful (if not more powerful) drive towards a standardized curriculum, and a return to more traditional teaching methods at this time in the UK, but initiatives such as peer mediation and circle time captured the imagination of many teachers, and were seen as a means of continuing some of the personal and social education work that had been sidelined elsewhere in the curriculum.

Stacey and Robinson (1997) describe the peer mediation services that they supported in several hundred schools in the early 1990s. The 'peer' in peer mediation either referred to a small number of students within a year group trained to offer a service to others of the same age, or to older students mediating younger students throughout the school. It sometimes referred to a team made up of students drawn from across the year groups. All students in school would normally have covered foundation work to develop conflict resolution skills, and would have had an introduction to the mediation process, before they nominated themselves or others for further training which took place off-timetable over three days. An intensive period of time such as this allowed for team building, proper rehearsal of counselling skills and for the students to develop their own guidelines for effective practice. Included in the training were the members of staff who would be supporting the peer mediators throughout the year, including lunchtime supervisors, learning mentors and teaching assistants. Although peer mediators had ownership of their service and made decisions about the way in which the service ran, they also had regular adult support and supervision. This support varied according to the age of the students involved, but all had a weekly team-meeting to debrief, to share experiences, and to keep up a regular programme of review and development.

When the services were initially set up, decisions were made about what sorts of problems were appropriate for peer mediation and about how to enable a maximum number of students to access the service. The finer details of rota and responsibilities for running the scheme from day to day were also considered (see for example Haigh, 1994). In many models, the service took place at lunchtime four times a week. Some chose to withdraw into a quiet room or private corner, whereas other services operated out in play areas at a designated spot (see for example Brace, 1995, who describes how the students at Highfield Junior and Infants school in Birmingham mediated under a tree in the playground). Stacey and Robinson (1997) found that peer mediation services are more likely to be well used when a high profile was maintained throughout the school year. In many of these successful initiatives teams of mediators gave themselves a clear identity, choosing names (Trouble Busters, Helping Hands, and Untanglers), logos, slogans ('release the peace and be strong') and forms of identification such as baseball caps, badges and sweatshirts. The usual stage at which students were trained to become peer mediators was at key stage two (age seven to 11) or key stage three (11- to 14-year-olds).

Cremin (2001) notes that there are both similarities and differences between American and British peer mediation projects. The main difference is that many of the American peer mediation projects are part of a wider community mediation service and have ongoing support. Many UK schools use school or charitable funds to finance peer mediation, and do not have this outside support. There is also a difference in focus. Stacey and Robinson (1997), for example, are concerned with pedagogy and developmental skills-training through the curriculum, while Araki (1990) is more concerned with the role of the peer mediation programme as part of a community-wide approach to dealing with conflict. The UK model also relies less on adults, and mediation occurs over lunch and break times rather than during the school day. Clearly, there are advantages in having an outside agency provide ongoing training and support, ensuring that the profile of the programme is high both within the school and in the wider community, but there are also advantages in a school being supported to take early ownership of the programme.

Research into 15 schools with successful peer mediation schemes

Cremin (2003) describes some research that she carried out in Birmingham in the UK in order to answer the question of why some schools are more able than others to sustain peer-mediation projects in schools. A similar issue of sustainability has been raised by Sellman (2002). The research was carried out at a peer mediator's conference in November 2001, which aimed to celebrate several years of successful peer mediation practice. Sixty peer mediators (aged from nine to 11) were present. They were representatives from 15 schools where, for a number of years, students had been trained in how to resolve the playground disputes of other students. The author was involved in setting up and running the conference in partnership with the staff and students of Stanville School, Birmingham (see Chapter 6). The day was particularly memorable for the mediators as both the chief education officer of Birmingham LEA, Professor Tim Brighouse, and the Secretary of State for Education, the Right Honourable Estelle Morris, attended part of the day in order to present the children with medals, which had been produced by the Birmingham Mint to celebrate their achievements. The day was made possible by a grant from Quest Millennium.

The main school that organized the conference, Stanville Junior and Infant School in Birmingham, is in Sheldon. Stanville, in common with the other schools, is an urban school in Birmingham with a mixed social and ethnic intake. The other 14 schools were invited to attend the conference on the basis that they were known to be operating peer mediation services in Birmingham. Each school was asked to send one teacher and three year-five students (Stanville sent 15 mediators). The teachers were chosen by the schools following an invitation addressed to the 'peer mediation co-ordinator'. Some of these teachers were relatively senior in the school, whereas others were just starting out in teaching. One or two were learning mentors or learning support assistants.

Three methods of data collection were used. Firstly, in order to gather basic information about how the services operated, one mediator per school was asked to stand up if a descriptor of peer mediation services applied to them. These are listed in Table 2.2. They were read out one at a time to the whole group during the morning of the conference. The activity took no more than ten minutes. The number of students standing up for each descriptor was recorded. Secondly, in order to elicit what the teachers felt had contributed to the success of their peer mediation schemes, a co-researcher carried out an unstructured group interview in which the teachers were asked a stimulus question while the students were occupied in workshops during the afternoon. The question was, 'What factors do you feel are responsible for the success of your peer mediation scheme?' The ensuing discussion was recorded and transcribed. Finally, students were also asked to fill in a questionnaire with mainly open questions asking them about their views on mediation more generally. There were 25 questionnaires returned from 10 boys and 15 girls. The questionnaires concerned eight of the 15 mediation services who were represented on the day at the conference. Table 2.2 shows the results of the activity, which

Table 2.2 A profile of how 15 successful peer mediation services operated in Birmingham schools in 2001

Description of service	No. (max 15)
Service operates in the playground	5
Service operates inside the school	10
Mediators wear badges	5
Mediators wear caps	5
Mediators wear tabards, sweatshirts or t-shirts	5
Mediators have produced a display with photos, details of the service etc. somewhere in the school	15
Mediators have done an assembly explaining their service	15
Mediators have met with lunchtime supervisors	7
Mediators have provided mediation training for teaching staff	7
Mediators operate a rota system for deciding who mediates when	15
Mediators sometimes mediate KS1 disputes	7
Mediators involved in more disputes between boys	5
Mediators involved in more disputes between girls	8
Mediators have had to stop a mediation because disputants have broken the rules	7
Mediators have carried out at least one successful mediation	15
Mediators have carried out many successful mediations	8
Mediators have used their skills at home	8

aimed to ascertain which descriptors applied to these peer mediation services.

Table 2.2 shows that successful mediation services have a high profile, with displays, assemblies and clearly visible ways of identifying mediators in the playground and around school. The array of badges, caps, sweatshirts and so forth that students wore on the day of the conference was a testament to the inventiveness and individuality of each group of students. Almost half of the services had involved the students meeting with all lunchtime supervisors and teachers in order to ensure effective communication. One-third of the services operated in the playground with two-thirds operating in the school. The advantages of having mediation inside and outside have been discussed elsewhere (Stacey 2000), but it is clearly perceived by the majority of the schools to be advantageous to have a room away from the hurly-burly of the playground. The rota system is well used as a means of ensuring that no students are losing too many of their playtimes.

The mediators who attended the conference were all in the penultimate year of their primary education, but just less than half of them operated their service for all students in the school. All of the mediators were being used, with opportunities for putting their skills into practice in real-life settings, and just over half of them having completed several mediations. In less successful services, mediators become discouraged when their newly found skills are not used due to poor take-up of the service. It is also clear that peer mediators were using their skills at home, which suggests that the skills had become fully assimilated. The fact that half of the mediators had had to stop a mediation because the disputants broke the rules suggests that the mediators had the confidence to assert themselves in a difficult situation and that they were clear about the boundaries of their role.

Table 2.3 shows the results of the discussion with the teachers from these 15 schools. The main elements of successful peer mediation schemes according to the teachers (student empowerment, a whole-school approach, resources, support of mediators, choice rewards and incentives, and social skills training for all students) are in keeping with earlier research (Cremin, 2001), in particular the importance of an ethos in which students feel empowered, and a whole-school approach to effective conflict resolution. The role of the headteacher is, predictably, central to ensuring a high profile, efficient and well-resourced peer mediation service.

The teachers discussed how they tried to empower their students. These teachers believed that their peer mediation services are genuinely student-led and that students have feelings of ownership and empowerment. Voting for mediators, and proper recruitment procedures such as filling in an application form and attending an interview with peers, were identified as ways that schools can both educate students for citizenship, and provide structures in which students can practise responsible power and control. One teacher summarized by saying that she tries 'to stay out of it'.

Table 2.3 Findings from discussion with teachers from 15 schools with successful peer mediation services

Elements of successful peer mediation	Teacher comments
Student empowerment	Student led Onus on the children Empowering for them Democratic Students elect the mediators Linked with voting system of school council Students deal with application forms, selection and interviews We try to stay out of it
Whole-school approach	Support of senior management Status and annual budget Part of school life Need to keep it going, can easily slip if not given high profile Hard if you are class-based Needs support from colleagues Needs a constant push You need to know the children Easier when embedded into school practice as the years have gone on Children know expectations of year 5 and 6, strong routines
Resources	Time / money / materials needed Trips important We meet with other schools for bowling, discos etc. The more mediators the better With 16 there is a critical mass
Support	They know that we are here for back up Fortnightly meetings to keep enthusiasm going Strict boundaries about what they should be dealing with Emotional pressure not too great Refer fights and bullying back to an adult 5 minute debrief at 5 to 1 before registration Need to get things off their chests. We do that every day
Choice, rewards and incentives	Some year groups need incentives Use computer suite to design reward certificates for other children Accept when children say they don't want to do it any more Need a get out Opt out clause at the end of every half term Contract makes it official

Elements of successful peer mediation	Teacher comments
Skills training	Need circle time in all classrooms to develop skills Year five class doing ten weeks of conflict resolution training to prepare them for selection of mediators Programme from nursery to year six doing circle time weekly in assembly time Class representative has a slot to feed into circle time Children develop skills to mediate by learning to talk about their problems in circle time

Despite the current overuse of the phrase 'whole-school approach', it is nevertheless the case that peer mediation needs the support of the whole school community in order to achieve success. These teachers listed several aspects of what a whole-school approach means in practice. Headteacher support appears vital. Expressions of this support included providing an annual budget for the peer mediation coordinator, and providing time to ensure that the service maintains a high profile amongst teaching and non-teaching staff. Status comes from the peer mediation service becoming embedded in school life, with clear expectations and routines. Difficulties in maintaining a whole-school approach include the feeling that there needs to be 'a constant push' and that the service 'can easily slip if not given a high profile'. Where colleagues are not supportive, a whole-school approach becomes more difficult. It also becomes more difficult if peer mediation coordinators are class-based and do not teach the mediators.

Resources, as ever, are identified as being essential to the success of peer mediation initiatives. Beyond the need for the proper training of staff and students (usually carried out over three days) the budgetary needs of peer mediation are mainly tied up in providing badges, trips and incentives for the mediators. Several of the teachers involved in this discussion had already formed links with other schools which enabled them to arrange trips and parties in common. The teachers spoke of the need for ongoing support and rewards for the mediators. Some groups of mediators seem intrinsically motivated with no need for any reward, whereas others seem to need other incentives. All of the teachers spoke of the need to provide opportunities for the mediators to debrief and feel supported by the adult responsible for the peer mediation service. Some teachers were doing this on a fortnightly basis, whereas others were doing it every day. It appears to be important that the mediators are also clear about the boundaries of their role. In particular they were told what sorts of disputes they should hand over to an adult and when their 'post' would end. One teacher stressed that it is important to accept when a child doesn't want to do it any more and another said that they have contracts in their school with an opt-out clause at the end of each half term.

The final area that the teachers stressed as important was the use of initiatives such as circle time (Moseley, 1994) to prepare the ground, consolidate and extend peer mediation services. This correlates with findings from previous research (Cremin, 2001), which suggested that the best possible strategy for preparing the ground for peer mediation was 30 minutes of circle time per week across the whole school. Circle time can be used to teach key personal and social skills such as listening, cooperation, impulse control and collaborative problem solving. Building students' skills in these areas goes beyond the development of effective conflict resolution practices. It also develops conflict prevention practices. Table 2.4 shows a summary of the responses relating to circle time, and who the students felt make the best mediators. The first column shows the question, the second the range of responses and the third the number of peer mediators who made a particular response as a percentage of the total responses.

Table 2.4 Findings from questionnaires completed by peer mediators from 15 schools with successful peer mediation services

Question	Response	Response (%)
Do you do circle time in your school?	Yes	100
Do teachers make good mediators?	Yes	68
	No	24
	Don't know	8
Do lunchtime supervisors make good mediators?	Yes	24
	No	60
	Don't know	16
Do parents / carers make good mediators?	Yes	44
	No	28
	Don't know	28
Do children make good mediators?	Yes	100

The responses to the first question, 'Do you do circle time in your school?' correlates with what the teachers said in their group interview, that circle time is an important aspect of life in these schools. The questions about who make good mediators are revealing. All mediators from these successfully mediating schools felt that children are the best mediators, with 68 eight per cent of them feeling that teachers are good mediators. Only 24 per cent, however, felt that lunchtime supervisors make good mediators. The students are perceptive in the reasons that they give for this, with issues of training and power featuring in many of their responses.

The majority of student mediators felt that teachers in their school make good mediators. One mediator wrote that 'teachers make good mediators because they are trained properly', and that they 'listen to you' as 'sensible good listeners'. These teachers 'usually sort out problems successfully and don't take sides'. Not all of the mediators, however, felt this way. One simply stated that 'teachers don't mediate at our school', with another suggesting that this is because 'they have not been trained'. Reasons why teachers make poor mediators include 'because they take sides' and 'because they solve the problem by shouting at them and sending them to a different class'. The powerful and punitive part of the class teacher's role is thus seen as a barrier to mediation, even in these schools, by some of the mediators.

Mediator's views about the mediation role of lunchtime supervisors echo the more negative views expressed about teachers. One mediator states 'they don't mediate' with another raising the issue of training 'our lunchtime supervisors haven't been trained yet, but will be later in the year'. The punitive aspect of their role is highlighted as a barrier 'they do the same as teachers (shout)' and 'they mostly give detentions'. Other comments perhaps reflect lunchtime supervisors' lack of status, low pay, difficult working conditions and lack of training and support in these areas:

> I don't think that lunchtime supervisors make good mediators because they are different kind of people.

> No, they don't. First thing is they are not trained, second thing is that they don't sort out problems – they chat.

> No, whenever we tell them there's something wrong they just ignore it.

Mediators' perceptions of the staff who care for them at lunchtimes are clearly a cause for concern. Lunchtime supervisors look after children for at least an hour every day in an unstructured environment where conflict can easily break out between peers. It seems counterproductive to train teachers and children in conflict resolution techniques if lunchtime supervisors are not equally trained in ways of helping create peaceful playtimes. Even in these successfully mediating schools, working with lunchtime supervisors could lead to a general improvement in children's experiences of conflict at lunchtime.

These peer mediators felt that parents do make good mediators, particularly when home culture matches that of the mediation service, 'they teach us not to do things that the mediators advise us not to do (name-calling, swearing, interrupting etc.)'. Parents were seen as caring and understanding, although some of the respondents felt that parents do not make good mediators because, like teachers, they have a punitive role 'no, because they ground us', 'sometimes, but they shout at you'. One mediator sums this up with a perceptive, 'well, some parents do, but some don't, so it's a maybe'. There was no equivalence, however, in the mediator's views about whether children make good mediators. Again, they relate this to issues of training and power:

> Yes, because children have been taught what to do.

> Yes, children don't ignore arguments and fights, and they are trained.

> Yes, they help and don't take sides, don't shout, don't tell other people, and don't tell them what to do.

> Yes, because we won't take sides, only children mediate.

This last comment can either be taken as a naïve understanding of mediation, or as a perceptive commentary on the nature of power relations in mediation. For mediation to be a truly empowering process, it could be argued, there needs to be an equalizing of power imbalances, not just between the child disputants, but also between the mediator(s) and the disputants. In other words, it must not matter (overtly) to the mediator whether or not the disputants reach a resolution. If the mediator has a stake in the resolution of the conflict (and teachers often do) then s/he cannot be sufficiently disinterested to be truly impartial. This is perhaps the strongest message to emerge from what these mediators say about the proper role of mediation in school, and who make the best mediators. One mediator puts it simply 'children make good mediators because they can mediate better than adults', whilst another states that 'children prefer to talk to other children', and another that, 'children make good mediators because they know how other children feel'. The mediators also reflect on the ways that the role of the mediator has enabled them to develop maturity beyond that of their peer group, 'it makes us more grown up', and 'once they (children) are mediators they become sensible and kind'. These schools have evidently had a high degree of success in empowering these students as genuine resolvers of playground conflict. This enhanced role in school appears, in turn, to have impacted on the mediators' feelings of self-worth.

The findings shown in Table 2.5 correlate with findings from elsewhere (for example, Cremin, 2001) about the most common types of disputes to come to mediation. Once again, it is the most subtle, indirect and psychological forms of conflict and bullying that appear the most amenable to the

Table 2.5 Findings from questionnaires completed by peer mediators from 15 schools with successful peer mediation services

What kinds of things do you mediate about?	No. of responses
Name-calling and swearing	15
Arguments	11
Fights	9
Friends falling out	6
Bullying	5
Accidents	2
Problems	1
Football	1
Hopscotch	1

Table 2.6 Findings from questionnaires completed by peer mediators from 15 schools with successful peer mediation services

What are the bad things about mediation?	No. of responses
Disputants breaking rules and being rude	10
Friends not accepting the role	4
There aren't any	3
Missing playtime	3
Safety worries	2
Missing football	1
Problems in the team	1

mediation process. Interestingly, these forms of conflict and bullying involve language, suggesting that students who access these services see language as both a means of generating harm and of bringing about resolution.

Table 2.6 shows that the negative aspects of mediation mentioned by these mediators centre mainly around managing their relationships with peers, given their changed role. This extends to both dealing with students who refuse to accept their authority within the mediation process, and to dealing with friends who can be resentful, especially as the choosing of mediators is often a competitive process, where not everyone who wants to become a mediator can do so. Schools embarking on peer mediation would do well to take account of these issues. Given these difficulties, however, the mediators felt that peer mediation has made a strong contribution to their schools. Table 2.7 summarizes the perceived benefits.

It is encouraging to see that the mediators focus on positive proactive reasons for mediation (school as a friendlier, happier place) rather than

Table 2.7 Findings from questionnaires completed by peer mediators from 15 schools with successful peer mediation services

How has mediation helped your school?	No. of responses
Less arguments	3
Reduced bullying	3
It is a friendlier, happier place	15
Teachers and lunchtime supervisors freed	2

negative, reactive ones (reduced bullying). This would imply that these mediators have a clear understanding of mediation as part of a whole-school approach towards social and emotional wellbeing. These successful schools have thus been able to transmit their core values to the mediators. Perhaps this, as much as anything else, gives a clue as to why these schemes have been successful.

Peer mediation schemes, then, need to be about more than tokenism if they are to thrive and last over months and years. They need to be founded on genuine empowerment of young people and a belief that disputants, with the support of peer mediators, really are best equipped to resolve their own conflicts. What is more, this belief system needs to be backed up with resources and a commitment to making peer mediation work. This entails time, money and training. It also involves all adults and children in the school community revisiting attitudes and behaviour relating to power and control. Peer mediation is not an easy option. It is not about abandoning a group of students to manage as best they can in the turmoil of playground life. It is about a careful and well-managed strategy for enabling young people to take a greater degree of responsibility over their own lives and relationships, with the full support of a dedicated staff team.

Conclusion

To conclude: mediation is a facilitative, non-adversarial process of dispute resolution that focuses on the needs and priorities of disputants themselves. Skilled mediators maintain neutrality, defer from making judgements and balance power between the disputants. It has the power to transform conflictual relations, and to bring about long-lasting settlements in a social world that is characterized by complexity, fragmentation and individualism. It is more interested in the future than the past, does not seek to apportion blame, and is not grounded in positivist, essentialist or statist views of truth, objectivity and justice. It enables genuine communication in a technological age where, although the volume of communication has increased exponentially, the quality of communication between human beings has not improved. Clearly, there are many cases in which mediation would be inappropriate, particularly where there has been a clear abuse of human rights, or where mediation is a substitute for the punishment of more serious crimes. Where individuals are able and willing to take responsibility for their actions, and to express genuine remorse, however, mediation can be seen as a valuable exercise for both the victim of a crime and the offender. Mediation in schools, where properly resourced and supported, can provide unequalled opportunities for young people to engage in the vital practice of effective dispute resolution, thus improving the quality of life in school, and preparing them for life beyond the school gates. As Baruch Bush and Folger (2005: 25) point out, 'The future of mediation is a matter of general and serious concern, because it implicates the future of an emerging relational vision of social life as a whole.'

3 The rise of citizenship education[1]

Introduction

Citizenship is a contested notion that has been interpreted and defined in various (often conflicting) ways across the political spectrum (Kerr, 2003). This has allowed citizenship to be used by those on the left, centre and right of the political spectrum in recent years (Faulks, 2000). Few doubt its importance, however, nor the significance of the public domain, which engages citizens with collective concerns. If citizenship denotes membership of various communities, then citizenship education equips young people to engage with those communities in positive ways. Democracies depend on citizens who, amongst other things, are aware of their rights and responsibilities as citizens; informed about the social and political world; concerned about the welfare of others; articulate in their opinions and arguments; capable of having influence over the world; active in their communities; and responsible in how they act as citizens (Huddleston and Kerr, 2006: 8). Democracy itself is, however, notoriously fragile, and where there is community there will be conflict. This chapter aims to show how the study of peace education, conflict resolution and peer mediation in schools are fundamental to the fulfilment of the promise of all that citizenship education has to offer. Any education for citizenship that ignores these core concepts is reduced in meaning, impact and relevance. A historical perspective on citizenship and citizenship education in the UK is given, starting with Marshall's welfare rights, continuing with Thatcher and neoliberalism, and ending with new Labour. International perspectives on challenges for citizenship education are given, including the demise of peace education, and the concomitant feminized values of care, non-violent action, and local concern for global issues. Potential solutions include the need to create new public spaces in which young people can respond to the decentralization of political power, and a reinvention of peace education, grounded in feminized notions of care and interconnections between private and public spheres of life. The chapter

[1] The author would like to acknowledge her collaborative work with Dr Keith Faulkes, who cowrote the conference paper (Cremin and Faulkes, 2005) on which some of this chapter is based.

ends by giving examples of initiatives such as Every Child Matters (ECM) distributed leadership and student consultation as ways of providing fertile ground for successful citizenship education and peer mediation. The findings from Cremin's research into peer mediation in three primary schools in Birmingham are given, and findings discussed in terms of the need to establish a culture of consultation and empowerment in order for citizenship and peer mediation to thrive.

What is citizenship education?

Huddleston and Kerr (2006: 9) note that, 'the last two decades have witnessed a fundamental review of the concept of citizenship and what it involves in communities across the world.' Their research into citizenship education across a number of countries shows that there is a common set of issues and challenges that the unprecedented pace of global change has uncovered. These include the rapid movement of people within and across national boundaries; a growing recognition of the rights of indigenous people and minorities; the collapse of existing political structures and the fledgling growth of new ones; the changing role and status of women in society; the impact of the global economy on social, economic and political ties; the effects of the revolution in information and communications technologies; increasing global population; and the emergence of new forms of community and protest. They conclude that, 'it is no coincidence that effective citizenship education has been included as a fundamental goal of education systems in the curriculum reviews that are underway in many countries. Schools, curricula and teachers have been given a significant role in helping to prepare young people for engaging with and participating in modern society' (Huddleston and Kerr, 2006: 10). This significant role is not without its challenges. For many involved in education, citizenship is uncharted territory. Its aims, objectives and characteristics are not always well understood, and its implications for policy and practice still only partially recognized (Huddleston and Kerr, 2006). There is a strong need to build on emerging practice, and to develop a more consistent and unified approach to citizenship education both in the UK, and elsewhere in the world.

Kerr (2003: 14) refers to a 'common tripartite division for thinking about citizenship education,' notably education about citizenship; education through citizenship; and education for citizenship. Huddleston and Rowe (2003) equate education about citizenship with the civics model, where the focus is on factual knowledge about structural and procedural matters.

This approach is the least problematic for teachers who have not been especially trained, as it can be easily assimilated into a humanities curriculum with a little background research on the part of the classroom teacher. He equates teaching for citizenship with the current affairs model, where the focus is on problem solving and topical social and political issues. This approach aims to prepare young people for their lives beyond school, situating them as future citizens who need to be able to engage in informed action and debate. He equates education through citizenship with the public discourse model, where teachers see the classroom as a kind of model public forum in which students practise public deliberation as a kind of rehearsal for adult life. Education through citizenship is the most challenging approach, but arguably the most effective, as it engages students early with the realities of social and political life, and enables them to learn key attitudes and skills through lived experience. It is to this form of citizenship education that peer mediation has the most to contribute. As Huddleston and Rowe (2003: 14) point out, each class of students has all the characteristics of a pluralist society in miniature (at least in theory) and provides the perfect training ground for young citizens, 'Each class of students is made up of different individuals from different backgrounds, espousing different beliefs and values, all sharing membership of common institutions and having a common identity.' Huddleston and Kerr (2006: 10) summarize effective learning in citizenship education as:

- active – emphasizes learning by doing;
- interactive – uses discussion and debate;
- relevant – focuses on real-life issues facing young people and society;
- critical – encourages young people to think for themselves;
- collaborative – employs group-work and cooperative learning;
- participative – gives young people a say in their own learning.

They extend these ideas on learning for citizenship by noting that there is growing consensus that effective citizenship teaching should be grounded in the 'three c's' of citizenship education: 'Citizenship learning takes place in three distinct areas of the life of an educational institution: through its taught curriculum, its culture and ethos, and its links with the wider community' (Huddleston and Kerr, 2006: 10).

As will be shown below, this first area of the curriculum is the least problematic for schools in the UK and elsewhere in the world, it is the other two areas of school culture and links with the wider community that continue to present difficulties for schools, and the social and political communities that they serve.

Citizenship education in the UK: a historical perspective

Citizenship has not always been a contested subject in the UK (Cremin and Faulkes, 2005). For much of the postwar period, until the election of the first Thatcher government in 1979, there existed a good deal of cross-party agreement on the form citizenship should take. This consensus was expressed in 1950 by T.H. Marshall in his now classic *Citizenship and Social Class*. Marshall (1992) argued that civil and political rights established before the end of the nineteenth century (such as free speech and the right to vote), were augmented in the twentieth century by the development of social rights. These were expressed through the creation of the welfare state, the national health service and public education, and executed by a growing army of professionals employed by the state to work towards the good of all. For Marshall, the inequalities of capitalism were both reduced in significance and legitimized by the addition of social rights to the citizenship package. This view is representative of a general consensus amongst policy makers in the postwar period in the UK that the values of citizenship are best taught indirectly, via the provision of a general liberal education (Heater, 2001). Building on the findings of the Norwood Report, which stated in 1943 that the teaching of citizenship 'can best be given incidentally ... through the tone of the school', citizenship education at that time stressed a civic identity that did not problematize the relationship between the individual and the state.

In the 1950s and 1970s, humanistic, progressive and child-centred education achieved many of the goals that are currently associated with citizenship education through such notions as empowerment, student autonomy and self-esteem. Influenced by writers such as Dewey, Holt, and Illich, a good number of teachers introduced active and experiential learning into their classrooms, encouraging students to take responsibility for their learning, and to see themselves as being at the centre of the educative process, rather than feeling marginalized by an impersonal education system (Cremin, 2001). Moves towards more active, child-centred, teaching and learning styles were stimulated and legitimized by the Plowden Report (1968), which emphasized the importance of children learning through discovery, group-work and discussion.

In the 1970s and early 1980s, peace education flourished in the UK, USA and Canada, and provided education for global citizenship. Peace education had peer mediation as one of its core activities. This was a time of nuclear proliferation, CND, and feminism. Many of the peace activists of the late twentieth century were women. Organizations such as Mothers for Peace (http://mothersforpeace.org) and the Women's International League for Peace and Freedom (http://www.peacewomen.org) were grounded (and continue to be grounded) in the desire of many women to work towards a better world for themselves and their children. Many hoped that peace education would result in more effective conflict resolution, locally and globally, and that young people would be empowered to bring about a more peaceful and just global community. There was a growth in numbers of peace education projects (for example, the West Midlands Quaker Peace Education Project, http://www.peacemakers.org.uk), new teaching and learning programmes (such as Prutzman, 1988), practical handbooks (such as Kreidler, 1984) and academic books and articles. Typically, these involved two interrelated strands: educating for peace and education about peace (UK Quaker Peace Education Advisory Group, http://www.quaker.org.uk). Educating for peace included examining the nature of conflict, and non-violent methods for dealing with conflict, as well as teaching children and young people the skills required. Education about peace included challenging widely held views and assumptions in society, as well as exploring topics such as war, conscientious objection, positive and negative peace, non-violent direct action, capital punishment and human rights. Active and participatory pedagogy was a strong feature of these programmes, with as much care taken over the process of learning as over the content of what was taught. In 1989, the United Nations Universal Declaration of Human Rights supported peace education as a means of promoting, 'understanding, tolerance and friendship among all nations, racial or religious groups' and saw it as furthering, 'the activities of the United Nations for the maintenance of peace' (Article 26).

Public sector growth, and commensurate increases in numbers of professionals, created challenges, however, particularly in the late 1970s. Citizens began to feel uneasy as professionals 'became increasingly prone to base their claims to professional status and professional rewards on their possession of technical skills, technical knowledge and technical qualifications that the laity did not possess, rather than on their commitment to the public good' (Marquand, 2004: 75). The UK's infamous 'winter of discontent' in 1979, which witnessed the Labour government's apparent powerlessness, set the scene for the advent of Thatcherism. Bamboozled, frustrated citizens and patronized clients would be reborn as empowered, liberated customers (Marquand, 2004: 75)! The implications of this for teachers are still being felt today.

At the heart of the Thatcherite redefinition of citizenship was the idea of market rights. These rights, such as property ownership, consumer rights, and choice between service providers, were seen as more empowering than Marshall's collectivist welfare rights. They were promoted through such policies as the privatization of public utilities, the introduction of market forces into the public sector, and the selling off of council houses. This way of viewing citizenship leaves little room for the promotion of other notions of social justice. Cremin and Faulks (2005: 1) note that:

> The active citizen of Thatcherism was a law abiding, materially suc-
> cessful individual who was willing and able to exploit the opportu-
> nities created by the promotion of market rights, whilst
> demonstrating occasional compassion for those less fortunate than
> themselves – charity rather than democratic citizenship was to be the
> main instrument of 'active citizenship'.

Marquand (2004: 2) describes the incessant marketization that began
with Thatcher, and has continued to a greater or lesser degree ever since, as 'a
relentless *kulturkampf* designed to root out the culture of service and citizenship which had become part of the social fabric'. For him, it has 'generated
a culture of distrust, which is corroding the values of professionalism, citizenship, equity and service like acid in the water supply' (Marquand, 2004: 3).
He notes:

> For the marketisers, the professional, public-service ethic is a con.
> Professionals are self-interested rent-seekers, trying to force the price
> of their labour above its market value. The service ethic is a rhetorical
> device to legitimise a web of monopolistic cartels whose real purpose
> is to rip off the consumer. There is no point in appealing to the
> values of common citizenship. There are no citizens, there are only
> customers.

Clearly, this way of viewing the marketization of public service has implications, not just for notions of citizenship (and therefore citizenship education)
but also for teachers as professionals in the public domain.

John Major's Citizen's Charter built on Thatcher's commodification and
individualization of social relations (Faulks, 1998; Cremin and Faulks, 2005)
but, despite the rhetoric of citizens taking active responsibility for themselves
and their communities, citizenship education was absent when the Conservative government created the National Curriculum in 1988. The one
concession to calls for citizenship to be included in the school curriculum was
the introduction of citizenship as one of five poorly implemented 'cross-
curricular themes' in 1990. As a result, many schools were unable to devote
enough time to covering citizenship education.

The failure to make citizenship core to the curriculum reflected the
Conservative government's mistrust of teachers generally, and those who
shared the concerns of the left in particular. John Major stated at the 1992
Conservative Party Conference: 'Let us return to basic subject teaching and
get rid of courses in the theory of education ... Our primary school teachers
should learn how to teach children to read, not waste their time on the
politics of gender, race and class' (cited in Chitty, 2004: 186). Teachers, so the
story went, needed to be brought to heel on behalf of frustrated parents and

exasperated employers. Marketization, as ever, was the intervention of choice. Real markets were not available, but ingenious proxy-markets, designed to force teachers and headteachers into the enterprise culture, were created with alacrity. Local management of schools (including financial autonomy), national testing of students at ages seven, 11 and 14, the publication of league tables, and the introduction of Ofsted, a government regulatory body, all contributed to a culture of audit, measurement and control.

Marquand has described the process of audit as an 'iron cage' for professionals such as teachers, restricting and constraining their practice. He argues that professional practices are necessarily opaque to those outside the profession concerned, and that professionals are people who have mastered demanding practices that outsiders have not mastered. He argues:

> By definition, then, external audit cannot judge the quality of professional performance in the ways that members of that profession would do ... The implications are disturbing. Since they cannot judge quality, external auditors have to construct a proxy for it; and the most convenient proxy is quantity.
>
> (2004: 111)

These 'disturbing implications', if accepted, are even more acute for citizenship education. Many of the outcomes of citizenship education (and indeed the humanistic, progressive and child-centred education that preceded it) are nebulous and hard to measure. As such, its market value for headteachers eager to show 'value added' is reduced. Many would argue that this is the reason behind the sluggish implementation of citizenship education in schools, even today.

By 1997, when the Labour government was elected in the UK, there was a perceived crisis in citizenship (Pattie et al., 2004) and in social and moral values amongst the general population, especially the young. The new government set about finding a 'third way' for citizenship and citizenship education. The publication in 1998 of the Final Report of the Advisory Group on Citizenship, chaired by Bernard Crick, and the subsequent government Order to implement its recommendations, has been characterized as a systematic attempt to provide, for the first time in England, the basis for a coherent approach to effective schooling for democracy (Kerr, 2003).

There appears to have been two primary motivating forces behind the introduction of compulsory citizenship education into the school curriculum at key stages three and four, and non-statutory guidelines for citizenship and PSHE at key stages one and two. First, the perceived growth in political apathy amongst young people, illustrated by low voter turnout especially amongst eighteen- to twenty-four-year-olds (Crick Report, 1998: paragraph 3.5); second, worries about anti-social behaviour, personified by the highly publicized, brutal murders of the black teenager Stephen Lawrence in 1993 and the London headmaster Philip Lawrence in 1995. Citizenship education would, it was hoped, help to create a more politically engaged and civil population.

David Blunkett (1998), the Secretary of State for Education at the time, outlined these expectations at the Report's launch:

> Education for Citizenship is vital to revive and sustain an active democratic society in the new century. We cannot leave it to chance ... We must provide opportunities for all our young people to develop an understanding of what democracy means and how government works in practice – locally and nationally – and encourage them to take an active part in the lives of their communities. Linking rights and responsibilities and emphasising socially acceptable behaviour to others, underpins the development of active citizenship.

The aims of the Crick Report (1998: paragraph 1.5) are ambitious, aiming at 'no less than a change in the political culture of this country'. Crick's three pillars of citizenship education – social and moral responsibility; community involvement; and political literacy – are grounded in the development of key skills and participation:

> Students develop skills of enquiry, communication, participation and responsible action through learning about and becoming informed and interested citizens. This will be achieved through creating links between students' learning in the classroom and activities that take place across the school, in the community and the wider world.
>
> (DfES, 2004)

This is all to be commended, although in practice citizenship education in the UK is yet to fulfil the promise of all that it could achieve. Recent reports and research from three different sources: the Office for Standards in Education (Ofsted, 2005), National Foundation for Educational Research (Kerr and Cleaver, 2004) and the Community Service Volunteers (2004) show that it is often poorly taught. It can lose its identity as part of personal social and health education (PSHE) and it can be seen as 'everywhere' and yet 'nowhere' in the school curriculum. It can be badly organized and coordinated, poorly assessed, and taught by non-specialists with little training or enthusiasm for the subject. Several commentators (for example, Cremin and Faulks, 2005) have suggested that this is partly due to an underinvestment in training, partly due to reluctance by government to mandate how schools should go about teaching this eclectic and politicized subject, and partly due to the way in which citizenship education was conceived in the original Crick Report. Cremin and Faulks note that the Crick Report (paragraph 2.1) situates its own position uncritically within the 'political tradition stemming from the Greek city states and the Roman republic' and are disappointed by the omission of more radical conceptions of politics offered by socialists and feminists, amongst others.

Feminist theorists highlight the fact that citizenship, like so many political concepts, has a gendered history (see, for example, Lister, 2003). Traditional male conceptions, such as those that dominate in the Crick Report, assume that citizenship is concerned with rational decision making in the public sphere. Emotion and care are confined to the private, non-political sphere of personal and family relationships. Citizens are viewed as bound together by rational, often hierarchical, social or economic contracts, rather than by a sense of interdependence and care (Cremin and Faulks, 2005). Noddings (2003) notes that traditional masculinist approaches to citizenship and politics often lead to conflict and violence in the name of some principle or another. Women (and some men), she argues, acting in accordance with feminized perspectives, 'can and do give reasons for their acts, but the reasons often point to feelings, needs, impressions, and a sense of personal ideal rather than to universal principles and their application' (Noddings, 2003: 3). As a result of this 'odd' approach, she suggests, women have often been judged inferior to men in the moral domain, and feminized perspectives have been ignored in the public sphere: 'One might say that ethics has been discussed largely in the language of the father: in principles and propositions, in terms such as justification, fairness, justice. The mother's voice has been silent' (Noddings, 2003: 1).

Citizenship education in the UK might have flourished better since its introduction into the National Curriculum if these more feminized perspectives on citizenship had featured more strongly in the Crick Report. In a similar vein, Osler (2003) regrets the omission in the report, and the subsequent national curriculum, of any critical perspectives on racism or international human rights. As Hoffman (2004: 166) has suggested, the thrust of the Crick Report is essentially statist. The danger of such an approach is that the divisions and inequalities of civil society, and thus the barriers to citizenship, are glossed over. It also misses the preferred political stance of many young people, which is to engage in protest and locally based or single issue politics (Cremin and Faulks, 2005).

There are also those who argue that New Labour's support of citizenship education conflicts with many of their other policies. They certainly have not gone about reprofessionalizing teaching with gusto. Marquand (2004: 124) notes that:

> Under new Labour 'the trust-denying audit explosion, which the neo-liberal revolutionaries helped to ignite, shows no sign of abating. In universities, schools, hospitals and social service departments, crude performance indicators, simplistic league tables, and centrally-imposed targets still undermine professional autonomy and narrow the scope for professional judgement.

Many teachers were dismayed when the new Labour government decided to allow Chris Woodhead, the chief inspector of schools who had been so negative about their profession under the Conservative government, to remain in his post for a further three years after their election victory. Writing in a Sunday newspaper in 2001, Woodhead described citizenship education as a new subject that merely serves to 'further overload the curriculum'. He described the fact that, 'Latin has given way to design and technology, citizenship and languages such as Spanish and Chinese' as 'a great pity'. It is perplexing that someone who was chief inspector of *state* schools for a period of seven years has lamented that 'state schools ought to be offering intellectual and cultural riches that are now, sadly, found only in the independent sector.' He now runs a chain of private schools.

Others have pointed out that the aims of citizenship education have been undermined by New Labour's erosion of the comprehensive ideal (Cremin and Faulks, 2005). Local schools have been replaced by schools offering greater specialization, selection and diversity in the name of 'choice' and standards. In a review of Labour's policies in this area, Taylor et al. (2005: 66) conclude that 'pursuing a programme of school diversity leads to greater social inequality'. As schools are encouraged to compete for students, better funded, popular schools can use their extra resources and admissions policy to select the most able and advantaged children. Current government policies will only exacerbate existing inequalities and exclusion by shifting 'major aspects of educational decision making out of the public into the private realm with potentially significant consequences for social justice' (Whitty, 2002: 87).

The ongoing marketization of education has more subtle consequences for students' perceptions of citizenship. The values associated with citizenship, such as cooperation, compromise and care are undermined when taught against a background of dominant market values such as competition, self-interest and materialism (Cremin and Faulks, 2005). Of particular concern is the encouragement of private sponsorship of schools. As Whitty (2002) argues, the 'hidden curricula' of such marketization forms the context that shapes understandings of citizenship and seriously compromises its emancipatory potential. There exists, then, a contradiction at the heart of the new Labour project. Its aims to renew citizenship are incompatible with its pursuit of Thatcherite educational policies in structural terms. These are the challenges that will need to be faced if citizenship education is to be more than a nod in the direction of civic renewal in the UK.

It is worth considering, at this point, whether the introduction of citizenship into the national curriculum in the UK is beginning to have the impact on antisocial behaviour amongst the young that was initially hoped for. It is early days, but it is indisputable that a certain 'yob culture' continues to flourish. Francis Gilbert in his book, *Yob Nation: The Truth about Britain's Yob Culture*, writes about his year-long journey throughout the UK interviewing both the perpetrators and the victims of violence, aggression and antisocial behaviour (Gilbert, 2006). Based on interviews with gang members living in some of the most deprived housing estates in the country, he reflects that many of these young people living on the margins appear to have no boundaries or morals, no empathy for other people's pain, and a desperate desire to be seen as tough and uncompromising. One of the lads who belonged to one of the gangs in Glasgow described the place where he met with the rest of his gang to 'discuss the business' of weekly fights with a rival gang. These fights involved bottles, bricks and sticks: 'This is where we have a drink, another drink, and then a smoke, and another smoke, and then another drink, and then another drink ... The lassies are not allowed here unless it's to get shagged.' The lad was 13, and had been coming to the same spot since he was nine.

Gilbert's strongest assertion in the book, however, is that 'yobbery' has become not just a problem of the young and the poor – the whole of society has become coarser and more violent. There are graphic accounts of violence, bullying and humiliation in the senior ranks of the army, the media, the city and international banks. Yob culture is seen as endemic in new Labour, with Alistair Campbell, Peter Mandelson, John Prescott, and even Tony Blair outed as power-crazed bullies. He reflects that modern British culture has created an arena where public streets have turned into battlefields, especially on alcohol-fuelled Saturday nights in towns and cities. This same culture is, 'highly materialistic', with every type of media from TV to the Internet celebrating the acquisition of costly goods – such as jewellery, trainers and designer clothes. It is also individualistic, with an emphasis upon the individual, 'achieving what he wants no matter what the consequences upon other people'.

Gilbert echoes here similar points to those that are made above: namely that culture and ethos in schools, and in young people's official and unofficial learning communities, are more shaped by wider social and political influences than are often taken into account in educational policy discourse. Discourses which view teachers as civic-minded implementers of programmes aimed at violent and antisocial students neglect the reality that policy makers and teachers are just as implicated in the reproduction of social exclusion and violent norms as anyone else. Young people are, arguably, more influenced by what they see in society and the media around them than by the overt curriculum in schools. In a society that allows those who have social privileges to exclude others, that values individualism and consumerism, and that favours those who are prepared to use aggression to get ahead, it is not surprising that bullying and 'yobbery' are so pervasive. The crisis in citizenship is, perhaps, deeper and more complex than new Labour bargained for when they introduced compulsory citizenship education into schools.

Citizenship education: an international perspective

Many of the conflicts and tensions in citizenship education, so apparent in the UK, are also in evidence in other parts of the world. The International Association for the Evaluation of Achievement (IEA) Citizenship Education Study was carried out recently in 28 countries (Torney-Purta et al., 2001). The main goal of the study was to identify and examine in a comparative framework, the ways in which young people are prepared to undertake their role as citizens in democracies. One focus of the study was schools, and the second was opportunities for civic participation outside of school, especially in the community. The study involved ninety thousand fourteen-year-olds as well as teachers and headteachers. One of the main findings, highlighted by Kerr (2003) is that, although schools that model democratic practices are most effective in promoting civic knowledge and engagement, an open and participatory approach to citizenship education is not the norm in most countries or for many students. There is, as Kerr (2003: 21) points out, 'conflict between the vision of citizenship education and its actual practice in most countries'. Although teachers recognized the importance of citizenship education in preparing young people for citizenship, and although they tended to have a vision of citizenship education that emphasized critical thinking and the development of values, in practice, the most frequent form of teaching involved transmission of knowledge through textbooks, teacher talk and worksheets.

The drift to the right in the UK, characterized by marketization and neoconservativism, has been witnessed in most other urban Western democracies in the world since the late 1970s. Debarbieux (2003) speaks of the 'urban schools market' in France where middle-class parents avoid ordinary schools to keep their social privileges. Following Dubet and Martucelli (1996) he notes that 'This game of choosing the "right school" ... questions republican egalitarianism much more than does violence from the victims of exclusion.' In this context 'Student violence is motivated by and is part of a process of protest and confrontation ... Students resist in several ways, more often violently, in order to reduce the grip of negative school verdicts on themselves' (Debarbieux, 2003: 23). Debarbieux here tips well-rehearsed social discourse on its head, with the young people who turn to violence seen as acting to regain self-esteem, control and dignity in an unequal education system that is doing 'violence' to them.

Writing about education and power in 1995, Apple chronicles similar processes occurring in the US, through neoliberalism. There are parallels in the ways in which the political right has engaged in a moral crusade against the public sector, including teachers and schooling, in the US. Apple notes:

> The political right in the United States has been very successful in mobilizing support against the educational system and its employees, often exporting the crisis in the economy onto the schools. Thus, one of its major achievements has been to shift the blame – for unemployment and underemployment, the loss of economic competitiveness, and the supposed breakdown of 'traditional' values and standards in the family, education and paid and unpaid workforces – *from* the economic, cultural and social policies and effects of the dominant group *to* the school and other public agencies. 'Public' is now the center of all evil; 'private' is the center of all that is good.
>
> (Apple, 1995: ix)

Neoliberal and neoconservative policies have, he argues, been 'more than a little successful' in challenging common sense, so that 'freedom equals the market, so that failure is only the result of individual character flaws, and so that democracy is simply guaranteeing the unattached individual a choice amongst consumer products' (Apple, 1995: xvi). The process of parental 'choice' undermining the values of citizenship, highlighted above in a UK context, is in evidence in the US, as is the role of the school in reproducing the inequalities of the communities that it serves.

Taking a neo-Marxist, Gramscian perspective, Apple challenges the traditional view of deviance in schools, where deviance is connected to some lack in character and motivation. Arguing that the process of schooling is not neutral, he maintains that, 'one fundamental latent social role of the school is "deviance amplification." That is, the school *naturally generates* certain kinds of deviance' (Apple, 1995: 38). Schools, he suggests, help maintain privilege in cultural ways by taking the form and content of the culture and knowledge of powerful groups and by defining it as legitimate knowledge to be preserved and passed on. It follows that the form and content of the culture of less powerful groups carries no such favour. Apple contrasts human capital theory with allocation theory, locating himself as an allocation theorist. Whereas human capital theory claims that schools are critical agencies for industrial growth and for mobility, allocation theorists assert the opposite, 'schools are not there to stimulate widespread class mobility. Rather, they basically act as sorting devices. They allocate individuals to their "proper places" within the hierarchical division of labor ...' (Apple, 1995: 39).

As will be explored later in this chapter, Apple is not asserting that students in school are powerless in the face of these social and economic forces. Students become adept at 'working the system' (Apple, 1995: 87) with large numbers of them creatively adapting their environments so that they can smoke, get out of class, inject humour into routines, informally control the pacing of classroom life, and generally try to make it through the day. Whilst Apple places these behaviours in the context of working-class struggle against oppression, they are ultimately fruitless and counterproductive. New ways need to be found to support the young and the disenfranchised to take power in more politically aware and positive ways.

The implications of all of this for citizenship and citizenship education have not escaped academics and commentators in the US and elsewhere. Kerr (2003: 9) reflects that, 'the review of citizenship has led academics and commentators to question whether a watershed has been reached; namely the end of modern, liberal democratic society and the onset of a less certain post-modern world.' Can citizenship education, grounded in modernist ideals of emancipation, collective action and altruism survive in a postmodern global age of complexity, individualism and uncertainty? What is the place of conflict resolution, peace education, and peer mediation in particular, in schools in a global postmodern age? It is these questions that will provide the focus for the remainder of the chapter.

New directions for citizenship education and peer mediation in schools

Far from the twenty-first century marking the end of the civic ideal, it could be argued that the skills and capacities of educated citizens are needed now more than ever. Willingness and ability to communicate, cooperate and solve problems will mark out those citizens who have a genuine contribution to make to peace at local and global levels. As Michael Apple (1995) points out, 'There's more than enough post-modern cynicism around, and in the meantime, conservative triumphalism litters that landscape with the tragic consequences of its arrogant tendencies.'

There are signs of civic renewal, with regeneration in cities, concern for the environment, protection of human rights, the growth of mediation, and many active and effective NGOs in the UK and beyond. A global public space, inhabited by a wide range of global political actors, is beginning tentatively to emerge. These signs of renewal, however, do not necessarily reflect traditional political concerns. Marquand, for example, notes the irony in the fact that systems of accountability and audit, designed to force professionals in the public sector to be more trustworthy, appear to have backfired on the politicians who have driven these systems through – 'the public seems to have lost trust in the marketisers more than in the marketised' (Marquand, 2004: 128). In a 2002 MORI poll, for example, 91 per cent of people who were surveyed said that they trusted doctors to tell the truth, 85 per cent said that they would trust teachers, but only 20 per cent trusted government ministers. Marquand (2004: 131) makes the point that, 'The picture that emerges ... is not one of cynicism, still less of apathy. It is one of street-wise disaffection.'

This view of citizens as disillusioned and disengaged is one that holds promise for new beginnings. Marquand (2004: 134) calls for a cultural shift that will develop, 'a new public philosophy capable of answering the now-entrenched orthodoxies of neo-liberalism, of challenging the all-pervasive ideology of consumerism, and of mobilising the public conscience in the way that the champions of the public domain mobilised it in the nineteenth and early twentieth centuries.' For this to work, accountability would need to be maintained through 'voice', 'ownership', and the principle of subsidiarity, whereby decisions on public policy are always taken at the lowest practicable level of government. This would need to build on 'wide-ranging, uninhibited discussion of the sort that command and control rules out' (Marquand, 2004: 142) and citizen's juries that would resolve disputes between stakeholders. Many of the themes of the previous chapter are reemerging here, and it is clear that mediation and citizenship education would be central to this cultural shift.

Apple (1995: 13) sees the education system as a significant area in which these kinds of positive changes can occur. Schools are not merely, 'institutions where the overt and covert knowledge that is taught inexorably moulds students into passive beings who are able and eager to fit into an unequal society'. Student reinterpretation, and often outright rejection of the planned and unplanned meanings of schools, can form the basis of enhanced criticality, if supported through creative teaching. Apple argues that students should be taught to act in ways that are counterhegemonic, in order to keep society dynamic and to lessen the grip of dominant political ideologies. Applying these ideas to challenging racism, Osler (2003: 51) suggests that, 'A new concept of antiracism needs to be developed, founded on principles of human rights, which recognises and is inclusive of a heterogeneous white population as well as those from black and ethnic minority communities who have traditionally taken a lead in challenging racism. Antiracist action and research need to be a central part of the project of realising democratic citizenship, and of citizenship education.'

Feminist perspectives on peace and justice are important here in reenvisaging citizenship and citizenship education. Feminized perspectives on peace tend to begin in the home and the local community, and extend outwards. Feminist writers offering new perspectives on human relations, psychoanalysis, ethics and moral education (for example, Gilligan, 1993; Noddings, 2003) have tended to focus on holism, and on links between the personal and the public, the local and the global.

Plummer's (2003) concept of intimate citizenship helps bring together a number of theoretical approaches that have challenged masculinist assumptions. Intimate citizenship renders issues that have traditionally been seen as issues of private choice and personal morality as directly relevant to the political world. In developing a systematic approach to the sociology of emotion, Barbalet (1998, 2002) has made a strong case for the premise that any social action, voting or carrying out one's obligations for instance, cannot be understood purely in terms of a narrow definition of rationality. The exercise of effective citizenship presumes a series of underpinning emotions, such as trust, confidence and security. Similarly, negative emotions of fear, envy and shame will seriously undermine the capacity of citizens to exercise their rights and responsibilities. This 'is not an argument against reason, only against the inflation of reason at the expense of emotion' (Barbalet, 2002: 2). Writing from the perspective of psychoanalysis, Samuels (2001) criticizes the neglect of the positive input psychological approaches can make to citizenship. An understanding of the emotional basis of one's political beliefs and prejudices can only help to improve communication across ideological, ethnic and class boundaries.

In outlining how one might go about promoting a more feminized ethic of caring in families, schools (and indeed any local or global community) Noddings (2003: 6) suggests that efforts should be directed towards the maintenance of conditions that will permit caring to flourish. Caring is a dynamic and interactive process. She notes that, 'How good *I* can be is partly a function of how *you* – the other – receive and respond to me' and that difficulties arise when, 'We fail to share with each other the feelings, the conflicts, the hopes and ideas that influence our eventual choices. We share only the justification of our acts and not what motivates and touches us' (Noddings, 2003: 5). These points reflect those made by Ausburger (1992) cited in Chapter Two, about the more communitarian ways in which traditional communities respond to conflict.

An ethic of caring is promoted by individuals who are able to enter into a 'receptive mode'. The 'one so engrossed is listening, looking, feeling' (Noddings, 2003:34). Apprehending the other's reality, feeling what s/he feels as nearly as possible, is an essential part of caring. Under these conditions, conflict is dealt with easily, using many of the attitudes and skills of mediation:

> It may well be that you care deeply for some plant, animal or environment in which I have no interest. My carelessness may shock and offend you. Now my obligation as one-caring is to listen, to receive you in all your indignation. I do not give way because of political pressure and the might of your lobbying, but I listen carefully because you address me ... All this is of variable importance, but you still matter more.
>
> (Noddings, 2003:161)

Along with the rejection of principles and rules as a major guide to ethical behaviour, Noddings also rejects the notion of 'universalizability'. She gives attention, not to the judgement of particular acts, but to how people meet each other morally. The actions of 'one-caring' will be varied rather than rule-bound, and whilst predictable in a global sense, will remain unpredictable in detail.

Noddings reflects on how this might relate to the process of teaching. The special gift of the teacher, she argues, is 'to receive the student, to look at the subject matter with him. Her commitment is to him, the cared-for, and he is – through that commitment – set free to pursue his legitimate projects' (Noddings, 2003: 177). For this to be applied to citizenship education, the student would need to be engaged, not in a predetermined knowledge-based curriculum, nor in a process of preparation for some future status as active citizen, but in a process of sharing, dialogue and review that takes account of the student as a fully-formed human being, with passions, legitimate interests and political motivation, here and now. In order for this to happen, schools would need to change – 'what I am recommending is that schools and teaching be redesigned so that caring has a chance to be initiated in the one-caring and completed in the cared-for' (Noddings, 2003: 182). This would enable teachers to provide students with a clearer role model of a committed, caring, intellectual and dynamic professional and citizen.

In could be argued that transforming schools in these ways would reengage teachers with the best parts of humanistic, progressive and child-centred education that were lost in the 1980s. Peace education, perhaps renamed for a twenty-first-century context, could reemerge from the political wilderness. Much was lost in the rejection of peace education at the end of the last century. Much will continue to be lost, if citizenship education continues to adhere to outmoded notions of citizenship. Peace education has a lot to offer to the study of conflict, peace and justice in schools, and could, perhaps, now be reclaimed in order to bridge the divide between 'soft' skills associated with personal social and health education and the 'hard' skills of active citizenship in schools. An unhelpful rift in schools divides conflict resolution in the private realm from conflict resolution in public and international realms. The former is dealt with through though PSHE and relationships education, and the latter is dealt with through citizenship and the humanities. This is not how young people think of conflict. It is also not how many women and people from traditional societies think about conflict. Peace education offers a much more holistic framework for thinking about issues of conflict and peace.

Those wanting to engage with peace education in the UK through the citizenship curriculum would not have far to look. There are several areas of study that are related to the study of peace education and social justice (necessary for the promotion of 'positive peace'). These include crime, justice, law and human rights, diversity and ethnic identity in the UK, pressure groups and the voluntary sector, war and conflict resolution, the world as global community, sustainable development and business, employment and trade. Dufour (2006) gives examples of areas of study that are integral to education for a safe world, including nuclear weapons, weapons of mass destruction, genocide, terrorism post–9/11, atrocities, torture, human rights and issues surrounding the Middle East and other conflict spots. UNICEF and UNESCO continue to be active advocates of education for peace. UNICEF describes peace education as schooling and other educational initiatives that:

- function as 'zones of peace', where children are safe from violent conflict;
- uphold children's basic rights as outlined in the Convention for the Rights of the Child;
- develop a climate that models peaceful and respectful behaviour among all members of the learning community;
- demonstrate the principles of equality and non-discrimination in administrative policies and practices;
- draw on the knowledge of peace-building that exists in the community, including means of dealing with conflict that are effective, non-violent, and rooted in the local culture;
- handle conflicts in ways that respect the rights and dignity of all involved;
- integrate an understanding of peace, human rights, social justice and global issues throughout the curriculum whenever possible;
- provide a forum for the explicit discussion of values of peace and social justice;
- use teaching and learning methods that stress participation, Cupertino, problem-solving and respect for differences;
- enable children to put peace-making into practice in the educational setting as well as in the wider community;
- generate opportunities for continuous reflection and professional development of all educators in relation to issues of peace, justice and rights.

(Fountain, 1999)

The seeds of these new beginnings for citizenship education are already in place. The IEA (International Association for the Evaluation of Achievement) Citizenship Education Study found that 14-year-olds generally believe that working with other young people in schools and communities can help to solve problems. They prefer to belong to groups and organizations in which they can work with their peers and see results from their efforts (Torney-Purta et al., 2001). In reflecting on the outcomes of the IEA Citizenship

Education Study, Kerr (2003) foregrounds schools as places that are very important for young people. They throw up problems that matter to students and provide opportunities for them to take part in 'real' rather than 'anticipated' actions, 'This sense of *school efficacy* (of feeling involved in improving things in the school) identified in the study may be as important a factor in future in future political behaviour as the broader sense of *political efficacy* (the relationship between citizens and national government) that has frequently been measured in research on citizenship education' (Kerr, 2003: 21). The generation of young people represented by the study's 14-year-olds appears to be gravitating to a new 'civic culture' that is characterized by less hierarchy and more individual decision making. The barriers to effective participatory citizenship in schools do not begin with young people.

The UK government has certain policies that are in alignment with its continuing drive for effective citizenship education in schools. There is a legal duty in the Education Act 2002 for local authorities and governing bodies of maintained schools to consult with students when making decisions on matters that affect them. The Department for Education and Skills (DfES) (2004) have published guidance on this in *Working Together – Giving Children and Young People a Say*. Citizenship education can be used as a vehicle for addressing the outcomes for wellbeing in the Every Child Matters programme, which is, arguably, the most significant policy imperative affecting children in the UK in recent times. David Bell, the chief inspector of schools stated in 2005:

> I would like to make the link between 'participation' in citizenship and the 'making a contribution' element of Every Child Matters. Making a contribution involves 'asking children and young people what works, what doesn't and what could work better, and involving them on an on-going basis in the design, delivery and evaluation of services.
>
> (Bell, 2005)

For these seeds to bear fruit, however, more needs to be done to ensure that there is greater congruence between the aims and goals of citizenship education and the political and social context in which schools operate. This will not happen by chance. New Labour's much-vaunted joined-up thinking needs to be applied here to setting the policy context in which citizenship education can thrive. Schools also need to be more active in ensuring that citizenship drives school culture and practice. Huddleston and Kerr (2006: 83) point out that

> Creating a citizenship ethos involves more than just drawing up a 'wish-list' of the sorts of values and relationships you would like to

permeate your school. It means imbedding these values and relationships in concrete practices and procedures – in particular,
through providing opportunities for students to play a part in deci-
sion-making, take on positions of responsibility and manage their
own learning.

School ethos or culture can be accessed, planned for, implemented,
monitored and evaluated like any other aspect of a school's work, and a more
conscious approach will be need to fulfil the promise of effective education
for citizenship.

Peer mediation as citizenship

It will be clear from the above that peer mediation has much to offer this
newly conceived notion of citizenship education. What is being proposed
here is a more complex, responsive system of school management and
teaching and learning, capable of taking account of diverse perspectives and
conflicting needs, and building on effective conflict resolution at all levels.

This resonates with complexity theory, and ideas on distributed leadership. Morrison (2002: 69) describes the 'leader' of complexity theory as
someone who moves beyond ideas of command and control, and even
transformational leadership, into, 'genuine democratic, distributed, trans-
cendental, quantum and servant leadership'. This involves addressing needs,
motivations and agendas of individuals and groups, and developing a sense of
community with shared power and decision making. It also involves
acknowledging that leadership is less about role than about behaviour, and
that leaders can therefore emerge anywhere in the organization, including the
classroom (especially the citizenship classroom). As Huddleston and Kerr
(2006) point out, even in primary and nursery schools, children can exercise
leadership and contribute towards decision making on a wide variety of issues,
including class and school rules, rewards and sanctions, equal opportunities
and bullying policies, uniform, homework and so on. They list opportunities
for student consultation to be embedded into daily practice, through group
discussions, circle time, class and school councils, questionnaires, and sug-
gestion boxes. Students can take on responsibilities both in class and in the
school as a whole through peer reading/education, running a school news-
paper/Web site, buddying younger children in the playground, assemblies,
becoming class/school councillors, visitor guides, recycling monitors, school
researchers and class monitors and, of course, through peer mediation.

The national curriculum for citizenship gives prominence to the study of
formal systems of conflict resolution, focusing on law and powerful global
institutions. Clearly, awareness of these national and international systems is

the entitlement of every child in the UK, but a greater awareness of attitudes, knowledge and skills for effective conflict resolution in their everyday lives should also be their entitlement. Grounding the study of conflict resolution within a context of individualism and formal legal processes is a risky strategy in an age of global and intercultural conflict, especially when urbanized Western systems of policing and law are themselves facing unprecedented challenges. Gearon et al. (2003) suggest that citizenship teaching should support students to explore which type of process – adversarial or investiga-tive – is likely to be best suited for different types of conflict, and Hartas (2003: 104) sees the development of social-cognitive skills and conversational competence in multiple social contexts as critical to effective citizenship education:

> Learning within the social context encourages students to take a dynamic approach to meaning-making. This can be achieved by taking others' perspective and interpreting their thoughts, clarifying expectations, negotiating the purpose of a particular task, and monitoring their own performance.

Peer mediation in schools enables young people to engage with what Coleman (2000) has called 'cooperative conflict'. Cooperative conflict leads to power *with* rather than power *over*. In situations of cooperative conflict, the dispute is framed as a mutual problem to be solved by both parties. This leads to minimized power differences between the disputants, and to enhanced willingness to work together effectively to achieve shared goals. Citizenship in schools, and peer mediation, can achieve shared goals through introducing more cooperative and power-sharing approaches to conflict. As Baruch Bush and Folger (2005: 81) point out, the main public value of transformative mediation is, 'the value of providing a moral and political education for citizens, in responsibility for themselves and respect for others. In a democ-racy, that must be a crucial public value.'

There are those who have argued that peer mediation in a school cannot thrive unless it is built on a culture of citizenship and empowerment of stu-dents at all levels. Cremin's (2001) research investigating the impact of peer mediation in three primary schools in Birmingham, UK, will be revisited at several points throughout this book, and this chapter will now provide an overview of the main research findings in relation to citizenship. The research found that school culture and ethos were central in determining the success or otherwise of peer mediation in these schools. It will be recalled that the research used student questionnaires and teacher interviews to measure changes in levels of bullying, self-esteem and locus of control, following the intervention of peer mediation in these three schools. The students were in year five (nine-to-10-year-olds).

In one of the schools (School One) all members of the school – staff, lunchtime supervisors and students alike – were keen to participate. There was also extensive training of teaching staff. The programme built on a negotiated, well-established, code of conduct and reward system, and students were consulted about decisions that would affect their daily lives in many different ways. The headteacher realistically assessed the starting points and training needs of the students and staff, and supported all members of the school community to review their attitudes towards power, control and blame. Students were able to practise personal, social and conflict resolution skills in real situations, and this led to a positive school culture. In particular, the headteacher had realistically assessed the starting points and training needs of the students and staff.

In this school there was a reduction in the frequency of students reporting being a victim of bullying, and there was a reduction in the frequency of students reporting bullying others. Types of bullying that appeared to reduce were physical bullying, teasing and psychological bullying. The only form of bullying that both students and teachers felt was resistant to change in School One was name calling, and this was the case both for those experiencing it and for those perpetuating it. Several of the teachers in School One, however, identified peer mediation as a strategy that enabled their students to deal with name calling in a more positive way than would otherwise have been the case. Student self-esteem appeared to improve after an initial dip, and student feelings of empowerment also appeared to improve. Students developed more negative attitudes towards bullying. After the peer mediation training programme, students had improved their ability to resolve conflicts, to give and receive positive comments, to cooperate, to communicate, and to listen to each other. By the time the peer mediation scheme had been running for two terms, they were beginning to transfer these skills to situations outside of the classroom, and many students had developed a high level of competency in these areas. Students with social emotional and behavioural difficulties (SEBD) appeared to gain a great deal from this approach, with all students benefiting from a general reduction in disaffection and aggressive behaviour.

In the other two schools peer mediation training was provided but no peer mediation service was set up following the training. In these two schools, the programme was limited and the headteachers appeared to overestimate the skill level of their staff in solving conflicts without confrontation. It also appeared that students were sometimes discouraged from talking about bullying, with victims ignored or blamed by some teachers. Structured lessons, teacher control, and playground supervision were used as anti-bullying strategies, and negative behaviour was at times excused on the grounds of supposed lack of parental skill and support. The code of conduct and reward schemes were still being formulated in both schools.

In these two schools there were no apparent changes in student levels of bullying, self-esteem and locus of control. This is perhaps to be expected, given that neither of these schools fully implemented the peer mediation programme. These findings highlight the importance of peer mediation building on, and helping to establish, a strong culture of citizenship in a school. Peer mediation appears to have been set against the prevailing culture of these two schools who failed to complete the programme.

Teacher interviews showed that, by the end of the peer mediation training (halfway through the intervention) the students in all three experimental schools were felt to have gained *some* awareness of skills for effective conflict resolution and to be partly using them in controlled situations. The skills seem not to have been fully consolidated or internalized at this stage, however, and in general the students appeared to experience difficulty in transferring them to other situations. In the main, the students in Schools Two and Three seem to have remained at this stage, with the teachers in School One feeling that their students progressed beyond it during the period when the peer mediation service was active, becoming competent in most of the skills and able to transfer them to other situations. Changes from a medium level of skill to a high level of skill were reported to have occurred mostly amongst the students in School One, after the end of the training period, suggesting that a high level of change was the result of students consolidating their skills in real-life situations.

Conclusion

Marquand (2004) sees the public domain as both priceless and precarious, 'a gift of history, which is always at risk'. He sees the private domain of love, friendship and personal connection, and the market domain of buying and selling as 'products of nature' whereas 'the public domain depends on careful and continuing nurture' (Marquand, 2004: 2). Noddings (2003) attempts to unite these divided realms through an 'ethical ideal of caring' which strives to maintain and enhance caring at all levels, but neither would argue that social justice can be achieved without a good deal of effort, and the actions of skilled and committed citizens. A national curriculum for citizenship which covers only traditional legal systems in the UK will not prepare young people adequately for the experiences of dispute resolution that they are likely to encounter as adults. Mediation as a process of alternative dispute resolution is set to stay, and to grow in popularity as it becomes accepted as an informal and commonsense model of responding to conflict. As such, peer mediation, far from being a 'soft' option suitable for study as part of personal and social education, is presented here as a viable response to the need to develop more diverse, complex and globalized notions of citizenship in schools. Peace educators have long seen this link, and have been promoting peer mediation in schools for over 30 years. Now is the time to take up their challenge, and to follow through on the promise of effective education for peace and citizenship in schools.

4 Peer mediation and inclusion

Introduction

This chapter is concerned with issues of inclusion for children with special educational needs (SEN) particularly those with social emotional and behavioural difficulties (SEBD) and the role that peer mediation can play in this. It reviews the shift from medical to environmental models of special educational needs (SEN). It is suggested that, despite the difficulties, teachers can and should consult with students with SEBD in order to maintain the health of schools as organizations. Behaviour management that is grounded in student-centred discipline and peer mediation enables student voices to be heard, rather than suppressed and marginalized. This is contrasted with authoritarian and behaviourist methods of discipline, which centre on teacher surveillance and control, denying students opportunities for developing self-discipline and a personal moral code, and denying schools opportunities for self-review, growth and renewal. Peer mediation is seen as an important strategy for helping to bring this about. The chapter ends by reviewing research into the implementation of peer mediation in a school for students with moderate learning difficulties (Warne, 2003) and the parts of Cremin's research from 2001 that relate to the impact of peer mediation on student-centred discipline.

The challenge of including all students in mainstream education has preoccupied professionals for the past few decades. It has not been an insignificant challenge. This is not because all students cannot be educated in normal, local schools, but because educational settings have traditionally been designed in such a way as to exclude some students. In some cases exclusion is visible (stairs that are impossible for wheelchairs to navigate) but in others exclusionary practice is more subtle and harder to challenge. The battle for inclusion centres around key structural changes, but perhaps more importantly, it also involves changing hearts and minds. As with citizenship education, it is as much a matter of whether policy makers and teachers believe that all children can be included as it is about finding the necessary means of making this happen. Significant progress has been made in including children in wheelchairs in mainstream schools, but children with social emotional and behavioural difficulties (SEBD) continue to face segregation and exclusion. Hard-pressed teachers, judged primarily on test scores and exam results, have (quite understandably) often raised the question of whether inclusion of these students is viable (Neill, 2001) given the impact of their behaviour on the learning of other students. Strategies to reduce this impact have tended to emanate from educational psychology, and have centred around teacher control, rewards, sanctions and surveillance. It is less common for student-centred methods to be used, certainly within the context of the peer group. Although students experiencing difficulties often work with a counsellor, support worker or mentor on a one-to-one basis, the interface between students' experiences in individualized or small-group settings, and their experiences in mainstream classrooms is often not well managed. Benefits to students can be mitigated by the vagaries of short-term funding, poor communication with teaching staff, and conflicting goals, values attitudes and working practices. Peer mediation, with its educative approach and grounding in humanistic, student-centred and collaborative approaches to behaviour management, has much to offer here.

This chapter will explore these issues, beginning with a brief overview of inclusion in schools. It will then focus on students with SEBD, before going on to show how child-centred collaborative discipline in schools can aid the inclusion of these children, as well as providing a structure for effective behaviour management of all children. It will provide a critique of authoritarian and behaviourist methods of behaviour management, and show how peer mediation can contribute to an alternative means of managing aggression and conflict in school. The results of Cremin's (2001) research into the use of peer mediation to reduce bullying will be explored here in order to draw out links between peer mediation and the reduction of aggressive and antisocial behaviour in schools.

Inclusion in schools

The last century saw an important transition for children with disabilities and/or special educational needs (SEN). As the century went on, the right of all children to education was increasingly recognized. In the UK, the Education Act 1944 had a significant impact, stipulating that, wherever possible, children with disabilities should receive some form of education, either within hospitals, junior training centres or special schools. Medical examination and intelligence testing had been widely used since the 1900s, and continued to provide legitimation of a medical model of disability. It is this medical model (as opposed to an environmental or social model) that has been so vehemently challenged by groups of disabled people, and other advocates of disability rights, in the past few decades.

The 1970 Education Act recognized the right to education of those children who had previously been classified as ineducable. There was a significant shift from locating their needs within health settings to locating them within education settings. The act ended the arrangements for, 'classifying children suffering from a disability of mind as children unsuitable for education at school', and resulted in some 24,000 children from junior training centres and special care units across England along with 8000 in 100 hospitals being entitled to education. As Thomas and Vaughan (2004: 123) point out, however, these children were immediately labelled 'severely educationally subnormal (ESN) and received their education at one of the 400 new special schools formed as a result of this law'.

The 1981 Education Act built on the findings of the highly significant Warnock Report (DES, 1978). This stated that all children with SEN should be educated in ordinary schools, provided the views of the child's parents had been taken into account and that integration was compatible with the child receiving the special educational provision that he or she required, and efficient use of resources for both that child and those with whom the child would be educated. The Warnock Report attempted to capture a much more fluid conceptualization of need, clarifying that children could slip in and out of need at different times in their school career, and that ordinary schools could respond better to this through greater flexibility. Warnock (DES 1978) highlighted three main forms of integration: locational integration; social integration and functional integration. The first two involve a child being educated in the same building as peers, but in a special unit. Social integration involves a child also sharing break, lunchtimes and extracurricular activities with peers. Functional integration is the only version of integration that involves a child with special educational needs sharing curricular activities with peers. All forms of integration are grounded in notions of 'normality' and assimilation, leaving schools largely unchanged.

During the 1980s and 1990s, notions of what is 'normal' and 'natural' were increasingly questioned. Excluding children, young people and adults from the mainstream because of disability or learning difficulty became increasingly seen as negative discrimination and a major human rights issue. On the international stage, the UN Convention on the Rights of the Child (1989) and the UNESCO Salamanca Statement (1994) both strengthened the case for inclusion in the UK. Article 23 of the UN Convention reminds politicians and educators that children with a disability should not be discriminated against, and the Salamanca Statement called for inclusion to be the norm:

> Regular schools with this inclusive orientation are the most effective means of combating discriminatory attitudes, creating welcoming communities, building an inclusive society and achieving education for all. Moreover they provide an effective education to the majority

of children and improve the efficiency and ultimately the cost-effectiveness of the entire education system.

(UNESCO, 1994, quoted in Thomas and Vaughan, 2004)

Demands for change at this time came from pressure groups made up of the disabled, people with SEN and their parents and supporters. They fought for a shift from medical models of disability to environmental or social models. The non-governmental organization, Disability Equality in Education, talks about the ongoing need to change the focus of support from special schools, therapists (speech, occupational, counselling), social workers, benefits agencies, doctors, specialists and educational psychologists to providing accessible environments and useful education, and to reducing prejudice, poverty and segregation (DEE, 2002). This shift can be characterized as a shift from a child being seen as 'disabled' by a physical or psychological impairment, over to a child being seen as 'disabled' by their environment. They argue that disabled children, and those with learning difficulties, belong (and have a right to the support) in ordinary classes, and that all children with and without impairments benefit from inclusion, which is an important component of quality education for all.

The publication of the UK government's Green Paper on special educational needs, Excellence for all Children, in 1997, just a few months after a landslide election victory, 'caused considerable excitement and optimism in the education world, particularly amongst those favouring a move towards greater inclusion' (Thomas and Vaughan, 2004: 130). The foreword by David Blunkett, Secretary of State for Education, was very much to be welcomed:

> Schools have to prepare all children ... That is a strong reason for educating all children with special educational needs, as far as possible, with their peers. Where all children are included as equal partners in the school community, the benefits are felt by all. That is why we are committed to comprehensive and enforceable civil rights for disabled people.
>
> (DfEE, 1997, Ibid, p. 130)

The report endorsed the Salamanca statement, and named the important 'social and moral grounds' for inclusion, highlighting the need for education to prepare all young people to flourish in their various communities as adults. It also, however, made it clear that special schools still had a role to play, stating that the government's approach to inclusion would be, 'practical, not dogmatic'. Segregated education would continue to be a reality for some, especially those whose parents favoured it. New legislation in the form of the Special Educational Needs and Disability Act 2001 further strengthened the rights of parents to choose whether or not their children should be educated in the mainstream (provided that the education of other children would not be adversely affected) and increased the obligation on schools to make reasonable provision to ensure that students with disabilities would not be excluded from the curriculum or physical environment, should they opt for inclusion.

It is certainly the case that a move to full inclusion would be problematic, not least because of the financial concerns and professional interests. As Thomas and Loxley (2001) point out, current funding arrangements mean that fixed costs of special schools do not reduce when a child moves into mainstream. As long as special schools exist for some children, large sums of money will be tied up and unavailable for mainstream schools to spend on support for inclusion:

> Under this system, while six figure sums of money go to pay for children at some residential special schools, those sums do not accompany those children if they move back into mainstream. Nor are they available as a resource when a mainstream school is on the process of referring a child in the first place: there is no offering such choices as: This child will go to a residential special school which will cost £100,000 per year. Alternatively, the £100,000 is available to spend on inclusive support in your school.
>
> (Thomas and Loxley, 2001: 107)

Rustemier and Vaughan (2005) found that very little progress towards inclusion had been made nationally in the period from 2002 to 2004. Indeed, one-third of local authorities had increased segregation of disabled students over the three years. There were 'disturbing, local variations in placement across England', with students with statements of special educational needs in South Tyneside 24 times more likely to receive a segregated education than those in Newham, London in 2004.

For teachers, the move from integration (which involved the child 'fitting in' with the environment) to inclusion (which involves the teacher changing the learning environment to cater for the needs of all children) has been significant. Additional resources, training and teaching assistants have not always been readily available. The paraphernalia and requirements of the medical model of SEN have been a hindrance here. As Thomas et al. (1998: 14) powerfully state: 'A central aspect of an inclusion project must therefore lie in the deconstruction of the idea that only special people are equipped and qualified to teach special children.' In comparing traditional approaches to SEN (which may include integration) with inclusionary approaches, Porter (1995) shows that there are clear differences in emphasis. The first places its focus on the student, assessment by specialists and diagnostic outcomes. The second places its focus on the classroom, collaborative problem solving and the quality of teaching and learning. The first involves a special programme or placement for the student, the second involves teacher innovation, and new strategies for adapting and strengthening normal classroom practice. All of this has workload and financial implications for teachers and is not to be undertaken lightly.

Inclusion and students with social, emotional and behavioural difficulties (SEBD)

If responding to disability and children's SEN in schools is fraught with dilemmas, tensions and political and financial considerations, then responding to the needs of children with SEBD is even more so. To begin with, some SEBD have been 'created' by a restricted curriculum, high-stakes testing, and cultures of audit and centralized accountability in schools. Cooper (2001) notes that there has been a move away from the kinds of experiential and student-centred approaches that are favoured by many children with SEBD, resulting in increased numbers of excluded and marginalized children. Peer mediation has much to offer to these students. Children with SEBD and attention deficit hyperactivity disorder (ADHD) struggle in classes where the teacher has been forced to return to directive whole-class teaching, and traditional methods of 'cramming' for tests and exams. Garner (1999) points out that these children are 'particular losers' in the marketized pseudo-economy of schools, and Greenhalgh (1994: 7) notes their vulnerability:

> In this climate, when children with special educational needs have become so vulnerable, those with emotional and behavioural difficulties are potentially at the most risk, not only since these children can be difficult to work with, but because of the potential negative impact upon perceptions of the school and its public persona.

In a similar vein, Fontana (1994) has warned that we run the risk of categorizing behaviour as undesirable or deviant in children simply because it goes against our own prejudices, social habits or professional convenience, and that we often condemn behaviours in children that would be perfectly acceptable – even desirable – in adults (such as the ability to show originality and independence, to speak up for oneself, to show determination and courage, to be humorous and iconoclastic).

There is therefore a current danger that gains made for inclusion in schools dating back to the Warnock report and 1981 Education Act may be lost, and that a return will be made towards a general feeling that the 'problem' of SEN (and SEBD in particular) is located with the individuals with those needs and their families, rather than with the institution within which they are educated. The current UK government's orthodoxy that good schools are ones that get good academic results – as well as meeting the needs of their more vulnerable students – is fraught with inconsistencies. There are widespread concerns that the more limited agenda for increasing 'standards' for the majority is being achieved in many schools at the expense of attention to (and tolerance for) students who present particular challenges (Gray, 2002). The desire for politicians to claim both the standards agenda and the inclusion agenda has left teachers with the impossible job of trying to resolve the irresolvable on a daily basis.

Social, emotional and behavioural difficulties have complex origins, which are exacerbated by a society that is orientated around notions of normality and uniformity. Fontana (1994) has claimed that challenging behaviour has its origins both in the social and emotional needs of children and in the ways that schools are run. She lists the main causes of challenging behaviour in children as learned attention-seeking, failures of attainment, poor self-concept, inadequacies of personal adjustment, social influences, negative group dynamics, limit-testing and the growth of independence, developmental/cognitive factors, and affective factors (those associated with both emotion and personality, such as extroversion and introversion, emotional stability and cognitive style). Origins of challenging behaviour from within the school include an inadequate curriculum, overemphasis on testing and formal examinations, teacher behaviour (including body language and voice tone, control and clarity) the quality of lesson preparation, organization and presentation, and the use of threats/rewards and punishments. Above all, the quality of relationships with students is an important factor in determining whether SEBD are successfully managed or exacerbated in a school environment. If students are viewed primarily in terms of levels and targets for achievement, then these relationships will suffer. It could be argued that there has been a shift, since the late 1980s, from teachers seeing themselves as teachers of children and young people, to seeing themselves as teachers of subjects. For some students this has had disastrous consequences.

It is not just individual students who have suffered, however. Those who argue for inclusion, also argue that it is vital that schools take account of the dissenting voices of students who are experiencing difficulties in order to maintain their health as organizations. It is interesting to draw on social psychology here. Kurt Lewin (1948) was the first fully to appreciate the previously underestimated influence of any group in shaping the psychology of individuals who are a part of that group, and his ideas have been applied to several disciplines, including education. Fromm (1970: 37) draws on psychology and sociology comparing and contrasting Freud and Marx to suggest that in the latter half of the twentieth century it was no longer the sexual drive that was repressed:

In present day society it is the other impulses that are repressed; to be fully alive, to be free, and to love. Indeed if people today were healthy in the human sense, they would be less, rather than more, capable of fulfilling their social role. They would ... protest against a sick society, and demand such socio-economic changes as would reduce the dichotomy between health in a social and health in a human sense.

It is perhaps going too far to argue that young people who reject schooling, or who exhibit challenging behaviour, are protesting against a sick society, but it is equally false to argue that these voices can be suppressed without any consequences for the wider school community. Greenhalgh (1994) has argued that excluding, containing and managing children with emotional and behavioural difficulties is no substitute for working with them in order to fully understand the roots of their problems, and for creating schools that are sensitive to the needs of all children:

We are summoned towards renewal, towards a more holistic pattern of connections in helping us to make sense of emotional growth and learning. The challenge lies in developing our language and under-standing in ways which acknowledge and reflect the meaning of children's dilemmas; which help us to return the humanity to our thinking and practice; which enable us to make effective use of our relationships and the curriculum; and which help us to provide responsive yet flexible services in a rapidly changing environment.

(Greenhalgh, 1994: 10)

Humanistic programmes, and peer mediation in particular, with their emphasis on building a positive self-concept, and on the importance of feelings, and the quality of relationships, offer a means by which all children, but particularly those with SEBD, can benefit from developing their affective and social cognitive skills. They also enable a 'feedback loop', which is essential in a healthy process of school self-review and improvement.

Behaviour management in schools

General good behaviour in school is usually defined and upheld by a school's behaviour management policy, which is of the key policy documents that schools are required to develop and review regularly. Stacey and Robinson (1997) identify three main styles of behaviour management: authoritarian, behaviourist and student centred. They relate the three styles to each other as shown in Figure 4.1. Students are able to take increasing responsibility for their behaviour as teachers use less directive methods of behaviour management. This figure also shows that in the move away from teacher-centred methods into student-centred methods, behaviourist strategies can be used as a middle ground where teachers and students meet each other half way to define rules, rewards, and punishments.

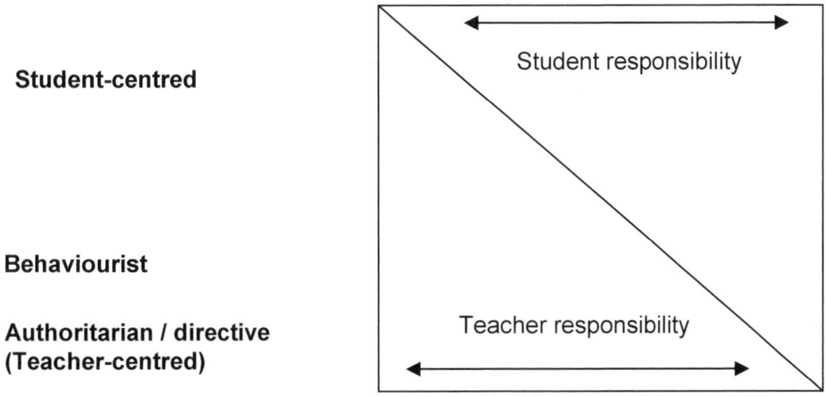

Student-centred

Student responsibility

Behaviourist

**Authoritarian / directive
(Teacher-centred)**

Teacher responsibility

Figure 4.1 Three styles of behaviour management in relation to teacher and student responsibility.

Source: Stacey and Robinson (1997).

Stacey and Robinson (1997) argue that all three styles of behaviour management have their place in schools, although they favour more student-centred methods in order to encourage students to take more responsibility for their own behaviour, 'We feel that adults who are serious in their intentions to help students become independent learners and confident autonomous young people, will be equally serious about changing their behaviour management style to suit and support their students' emerging independence ...' (Stacey and Robinson, 1997: 17).

Authoritarian methods, although providing the necessary boundaries for safety in school, can be counterproductive if they are relied on exclusively. Fontana (1994) argues that the disadvantages of authoritarian methods are that students, and often staff, are excluded from the process of making and maintaining the rules, and that punishment inhibits the development of a positive teacher-student relationship. In addition, punishment rarely encourages students to change their behaviour (other than learning to be more proficient at not getting caught) and does not encourage young people to behave well when they are out of the punisher's influence. For these reasons, Maines and Robinson (1993) propose that punishments should be as mild as possible. Mild punishments, they suggest, are equally as effective in behaviour management as more serious punishments and are not as damaging to student-teacher relationships. Finally, in punishing, teachers often model the kind of behaviour of which they say they disapprove. The importance of adults modelling the behaviour they seek to develop in young people is borne out in research by Moore and Eisenberg (1984) who found that, in experiments where children were exposed to a model whom they experienced as nurturing, prosocial behaviour was emulated. Where the model was not experienced as nurturing, this behaviour was not emulated, despite the children being told to act pro-socially. Sandy & Cochran (2000) argues that children learn in the context of important relationships, and that where adults model care-giving, they are able to promote empathy and perspective-taking amongst young people. Stacey et al. (1997) relate this idea to bullying, arguing that children learn more from observing adult behaviour than from listening to adult instructions. If key adults respond to a child who has been bullying by using authoritarian behaviour management strategies that rely on humiliation, shouting or verbal aggression then the cycle of negative behaviour is reinforced. Behaviour management strategies need to be clear, just and assertive in order to be effective. They need to recognize the right to teach, the right to learn, and the right to be treated with respect. As Osler and Starkey (2005) point out, for schools to be genuinely inclusive, they need to turn away from their authoritarian traditions and apply democratic principles to the process of teaching, learning and behaviour management.

Behaviourist methods of behaviour management can be equally damaging if relied on exclusively, and if used in ways that are overly punitive. They can be useful in supporting teachers to focus less on negative behaviour, and more on positive behaviour, and they can provide consistency and structure in chaotic classrooms but they also limit the development of self-discipline and problem-solving skills. Behaviourist methods (for example, Cantor, 1989) have grown out of experiments on animals, most famously Pavlov's dogs (classical conditioning) and Skinner's rats (operant conditioning). These experiments entail the manipulation of rewards and punishments to encourage desirable behaviour.

There are those who argue that the use of behaviourist methods on children is unethical (for example, Hall and Hall, 1988). Rogers and Freiberg (1994) oppose the use of external rewards and punishments altogether. They argue that 'fixed consequences' for undesirable behaviour, used in many behaviourist programmes, operate as if all students were the same, with identical needs and intent. They suggest that consequences for undesirable behaviour should be rational, 'Unlike fixed consequences, rational consequences have the students try to undo what has been done. If a student spills something, then he or she knows to clean it up. Placing a child's name on the board, or adding a check, does little to remedy the situation' (Rogers and Freiberg, 1994: 239). Learning, they feel, should be intrinsically motivating. This, of itself, is sufficient to ensure a positive learning environment, 'Learning that is interesting and comes from the learner requires no external incentives. Learning that is boring and is externally determined seems to require enhanced external rewards to keep a minimal level of student engagement' (Rogers and Freiberg, 1994: 234). They go on to argue that, although self-discipline is what most teachers would say they are aiming for, the methods they use to achieve it may well be counterproductive:

> Too often the co-operation teachers seek from students in order to teach does not allow for real engagement in the learning process. Teachers find themselves imposing their requirements for order without relating them to student requirements for learning. Discipline becomes mandated rather than developed.
>
> (Rogers and Freiberg, 1994: 221)

In imposing discipline, they suggest, teachers deny students the opportunity to develop an internalized set of behavioural norms. Self-discipline requires a learning environment that nurtures opportunities to learn from one's experiences – including mistakes – and to reflect on these experiences. As discussed in previous chapters, the effects of neoliberalism, neoconservativism and the marketization of schools and schooling have resulted in less autonomy for teachers and students in schools, an increased need for behaviourist methods of discipline and control, and a reduction in time and space for developing these kinds of internalized behaviour norms amongst young people. Powerful psychological tools (the human equivalent of electric shocks and food pellets) are used to impose order amongst young people who are increasingly required to engage in boring test-driven activities in school. Whilst it may be possible to impose order using these methods, it does not necessarily follow that schools are justified in using them.

Robinson and Maines (1995) contest the validity of assertive discipline (Cantor, 1989) which has been the most widely used behaviourist programme in the UK, pointing out that when a student gets a maths problem wrong, a teacher's first strategy is to teach. When it is the behaviour that is wrong, the tendency is to criticize or punish. Although many reviews of assertive discipline are positive (for example, Melling and Swinson, 1995), Dore (1994) points out that a growing number of critics accuse Cantor of inhumanity through seeking control by humiliation. Such critics (for instance, Martin, 1994) highlight the fact that assertive discipline assumes that it is the child (and sometimes the parent) who has the problem, never the teacher. Dore

(1994: 2) quotes Dennis Lawrence, a former senior educational psychologist, who saw assertive discipline in action in Australia, 'Classes are quiet. You can't hear the kids' voices. When they go outside all Hell is let loose. It's a pretty dangerous business. You are controlling their behaviour and not teaching anything. You aren't helping kids to come to terms with their problems.'

Unlike authoritarian and behaviourist methods, student-centred behaviour management does not rely on adult surveillance and control. As the term itself suggests, student-centred methods of behaviour management have their roots in person-centred humanistic psychology. Rogers and Freiberg (1994: 239–40) define the person-centred classroom as follows:

> Person-centred classroom management advances the facilitative conditions needed to encourage active participation in a co-operative learning environment ... Person-centred classrooms emphasise caring, guidance, co-operation, and the building of self-discipline that is developmentally appropriate for all members of the classroom. Person-centred classrooms encourage students to think for themselves and help each other.

Student-centred behaviour management is enabled by teachers establishing a cooperative classroom environment, and by developing students' reflective skills and ability to change their own behaviour. This developmental activity is often missing, with many schools having high expectations of student behaviour, without considering the means by which this will be achieved. As Stacey et al. (1997) suggest, 'In our anxiety to "stamp out" undesirable behaviour and qualities, we may invest too little of our time and energy in helping our ... students to learn desirable ones.'

Critically, student-centred discipline involves an equalizing of power between the teacher and the student. The quest for discipline imposed by teachers becomes the quest for self-discipline sought by students. Rogers and Freiberg (1994: 240) compare discipline in teacher-centred and person-centred (student-centred) classrooms, as shown in Table 4.1. For Rogers and Freiberg, a humanistic classroom is a place where the need for behaviour management recedes as students are routinely treated with respect, given control over their own learning, and encouraged to develop self-discipline through negotiating rules and reflecting on their own behaviour. Student-centred strategies for teaching and learning create the psychological space for students to think through the consequences of their behaviour in a supportive environment, and to take more responsibility for their actions. In so doing, students develop a set of internalized behavioural norms, which they are able to evaluate and adapt as circumstances change. In psychological terms, student-centred discipline therefore develops an internal locus of

Table 4.1 Rogers and Freiberg's (1994) comparison of discipline in teacher-centred and person-centred classrooms

Teacher-centred Classrooms	Person-centred Classrooms
Teacher is the sole leader	Leadership is shared
Management is a form of oversight	Management is a form of guidance
Teacher takes responsibility for all the paperwork and organisation	Students are facilitators for the operations of the classroom
Discipline comes from the teacher	Discipline comes from the self
A few students are the teacher's helpers	All students have the opportunity to become an integral part of the management of the classroom.
Teacher makes the rules	Rules are developed by the teacher and students in the form of a classroom contract
Consequences are fixed for all students	Consequences reflect individual differences
Rewards are mostly extrinsic	Rewards are mostly intrinsic
Students are allowed limited responsibilities	Students share in classroom responsibilities
Few members of the community enter the classroom.	Partnerships are formed with business and community groups to enrich and broaden the learning opportunities of students.

control and leaves self-esteem intact. These attitudes and skills provide a firm basis for peer mediation. Schaps and Solomon (1990: 40) found that this kind of developmental discipline brought about real benefits for students in seven primary schools in California:

> It helped them to improve social competence, interpersonal beha-
> viour . . . and understanding, endorsement of democratic values, and
> high level reading comprehension. They also reported themselves to
> be significantly less lonely in class and less socially anxious. Overall
> we believe the programme is fostering a healthy balance between the
> tendencies to attend to their own needs and to attend to the needs
> and rights of others.

It is useful to reflect here on the links between developmental psychology and the student-centred behaviour management that is being advocated here as a basis for peer mediation. This reflection should acknowledge, however, that many key theorists in this area have been heavily criticized. Piaget's (1950) contention that the stages of cognitive development follow a pre-determined order has been much analysed and discussed. Meadows (1988), for example, highlights the fact that training can accelerate progress through Piaget's stages, and Turiel (1966) has also shown that, under certain conditions, exposing young people to moral arguments one stage above their own level of reasoning can lead to an increase in their level of moral judgement. It is nevertheless possible to work on a basic principle that young people generally progress (at varying rates) through developmental stages, and that this progress is determined by both within-child and environmental factors.

According to Piaget (1950) children pass from 'the concrete operational stage' into the 'formal operational stage', and thus become increasingly able to handle hypotheses and abstract concepts. The ability to understand perspectives that may be unfamiliar, and empathize with others, are central to student-centred behaviour management and to mediation. Preschool children appear to understand friendship in terms of physical characteristics: who they spend the most time with or live nearest to. Selman's research (1980) and extensive studies by Berndt (1983, 1986) show that in the primary school (four-to-11-year-olds) these views change to an ever-greater focus on reciprocal trust. Friends increasingly become special people who have qualities other than mere proximity. In adolescence, Berndt finds a further change towards greater mutual understanding. Friendships become more intense, long term, and exclusive.

Moral reasoning and the ability to empathize are also key to both student-centred discipline and mediation. Hoffman (1982, 1988) has identified stages in the development of empathy, suggesting that, although children as young as two or three may be able to respond to another's feelings in non-egocentric ways, over the primary years children learn to distinguish a wider and wider range of emotions, with empathy for another's life condition beginning in late childhood or early adolescence. According to Piaget (1950) children's moral reasoning progresses from heteronymous morality (moral realism) to autonomous morality (the morality of reciprocity). Children of primary-school age move from believing in absolute right and wrong to seeing social rules as arbitrary and changeable, with the intent of the person performing an action important in judging its morality. Piaget also argued that they change from believing in immanent justice (if they break a rule, punishment will inevitably follow) to understanding that rule violations do not result in inevitable punishment.

Kohlberg's (1976) description of moral development overlaps that of Piaget, but is more flexible and extends into adolescence and adulthood. People who are in Kohlberg's stage of pre-conventional morality decide what is right and wrong on the basis of reward and punishment. Those who are in the conventional stage of morality make judgements on the basis of mutual expectations agreed in the family or in society at large. Those who are in the principled or post-conventional stage (and many adults do not reach this stage) make judgements on the basis of the rights of the individual and the greater good of humanity. At this stage, conscience dominates over law, and the individual has a consistent system of ethical values.

What emerges from these theories of human development, regardless of the ways in which the various stages are conceptualized, is that young people generally progress from a self-centred, concrete and absolute view of the world to a stance that entails greater complexity, reciprocity, empathy and relativism. This natural process can be enabled or hindered by environmental factors, such as exposure to opportunities for moral reasoning. It could be argued that one of the most important roles that schools can play is to support the development of a personal moral code, self-discipline and an internalized set of behavioural norms. This is of benefit to both individual young people and society at large. Student-centred discipline and mediation support young people to achieve mature, autonomous concepts of justice through cooperation, reciprocity, and role taking. The absence of an absolute authority figure enables children to develop ideas of equality, cooperation, and group solidarity. Teacher-centred discipline denies young people opportunities to engage in these processes, doing their 'work' for them, unnecessarily prolonging early concrete and absolutist stages of moral development, and delaying moral maturity.

Sandy and Cochran (2000) give an example of how children's moral development can be enhanced through a programme designed to support the development of social and affective skills. Drawing on neuroscience, they argue that children get 'smarter' as they interact with the environment; but that 'Children who do not pass key emotional developmental milestones are at risk of retaining negative traits, such as impulsivity, immature emotional functioning, behavioural problems, and propensity to violence' (Sandy and Cochran, 2000: 324). To combat this, they have developed the Peaceful Kids Early Childhood Social-Emotional Learning (ECSEL) curriculum through Teachers' College, Columbia University (Sandy and Cochran, 1998). This involves providing children with opportunities to develop: vocabulary related to feelings, cooperation and problem solving; cooperative discipline techniques; and mutual affection and trust between teachers, parents and children. In this way, 'the accent is on helping the child understand both her own and the other person's feelings and perspective, as well as the consequences of her action, rather than simply getting the child to obey' (Sandy and Cochran, 2000: 328).

Student-centred behaviour management provides an environment in which students can review the negative effects of their behaviour whilst feeling valued and accepted by their teacher and peers. It focuses on the development of an internalized moral code and set of behavioural norms, and encourages an internal locus of control. It requires students to develop certain values, attitudes and social cognitive skills and it requires teachers to provide the necessary psychological space for this to happen. More directive behaviour management, such as authoritarian and behaviourist methods, may well be necessary to maintain student safety in certain cases, but the adverse effects of punishment, and even of extrinsic rewards, limit their effectiveness.

Peer mediation, inclusion and behaviour management

It will be clear from the above that schools who operate largely behaviourist or authoritarian regimes will experience some difficulties in successfully implementing peer mediation. The remainder of this chapter will focus on the ways in which peer mediation can build on inclusion and student-centred discipline in schools. It will report on some findings from research into peer mediation in a special school (Warne, 2003) before expanding on the findings of the research into peer mediation in three primary schools reported in Chapter Three (Cremin, 2001).

Warne (2003) developed and evaluated a peer mediation scheme in a special school for students with moderate learning difficulties (MLD). She was PHSE/citizenship coordinator in the school at the time. The project was introduced in order to support students to deal with low-level peer conflict, quarrels, name calling and minor disputes. Warne was also concerned to use peer mediation, and the additional responsibility that this involves, to improve the self-esteem, social skills and emotional literacy of the students in the school. The training of the peer mediators covered cooperation, communication, positive emotional expression, appreciation of diversity and conflict resolution skills. The students were taken off site for a full training day, and this was then followed up with five half days spread over several weeks. All skills were reinforced by class teachers during circle time, and through other curricular activities.

Peer mediators were selected from every tutor group, ensuring proper representation. They were selected according to their commitment, reliability and their popularity with peers, and according to their general ability to understand, articulate and evaluate peer conflict, and to maintain confidentiality. The whole school community was involved with the project, with teaching staff, learning support assistants, the caretaker, the kitchen and office staff, the lunchtime supervisors and the governors of the school included to varying degrees. The training for the students was carried out by a qualified and experienced counsellor helped by sixth formers from a local school.

Interviews were carried out with the trainers and the mediators to ascertain the effectiveness of the training. The students said that they had learnt:

- to help people who are arguing (including people at home);
- not to get involved with physical fighting;
- to keep themselves safe – when to ask for help from a teacher;
- to sort out problems;
- to approach problems differently and work though a set process;
- to help other members of the team;
- to talk to people more, and to listen better;
- to look at people when listening;
- how to stop people fighting.

Arora's *Life in School Checklist* (1994) was used to measure changes in positive and negative experiences in school, before, during and after the peer-mediation project. The questionnaire was completed by all students in the school on three occasions. Findings suggest that low-level conflict and bullying were reduced following the peer-mediation project, although Warne is sceptical of some of the statistics due to the small sample size, the MLD of some of the students completing the questionnaires, and the fact that not all students completed all three of the questionnaires. She is also concerned that participating in the research may have altered staff and student responses. These findings were, however, augmented by observations of students, and anecdotal evidence from teaching and non-teaching staff. Observations of students during break and lunchtimes suggested a greater cooperative atmosphere, with six of the mediators being seen mediating effectively, two working behind the scenes, and four less active. Anecdotal evidence included several incidents of peer mediators intervening early where peers might otherwise have got into trouble.

The peer mediators themselves felt that there was a general improvement in the cooperative atmosphere in school. They felt that their peers were beginning to be aware of other ways of resolving difficulties, not just aggressive confrontation. Some of the mediators felt that improvements had occurred elsewhere, such as on the school buses. They were particularly pleased about the increased respect that was shown to them by peers and staff and they liked the feeling of being part of a successful and dynamic team. Half of them were confident to use the mediation process but those who were less confident were able to identify other ways in which being part of the team had helped them with friendship and empathy.

This research makes it clear that peer mediation can be used with students with MLD, and that it can be a powerful tool in improving cooperation, communication, self-esteem and conflict-resolution skills amongst mediators and mediated. Although the process of mediating involves a number of steps, and although some of the concepts are fairly complex, it is clear that students of all abilities can benefit from a peer-mediation project. Warne relates the success of this project to a whole-school approach, a supportive headteacher,

her own role as a committed and reflective practitioner, and practical elements such as off-site training (to mark it out as special) adapting teaching materials and activities to cater for the learning needs of students, and ensuring ownership through enabling the mediators to choose their own name, badge design, duty rota, and so forth. She ends her paper by stating that her project shows that:

> Mediation is not dependent on intellectual ability, but on the ability to listen, to empathise without making judgements, and having the desire to help others solve problems. Many of our pupils developed and adapted their own way of mediating depending on their level of ability. The introduction of the project played a notable part in increasing cooperation between pupils ...
>
> (Warne, 2003: 32–3)

It will be recalled that in Cremin's (2001) research into peer mediation in three primary schools in Birmingham the project was only fully implemented in School One, with Schools Two and Three engaging in the training programme but not the actual practice of peer mediation. In some ways this failed experiment provided useful insights, demonstrating the importance of young people trying out newly acquired social cognitive skills rather than just learning about them. The research showed that where teaching is based on games and hypothetical situations, partial learning seems to take place but young people are left without the ability to transfer learning to new situations. A case in point is the progress that the students appeared to make between the end of the training programme and the end of the full implementation of peer mediation in School One. During the second interviews (which took place when the peer mediation training programme was complete) one of the teachers stated that her students' skills of conflict resolution, communication, affirmation, cooperation, listening, and mediation were, 'pretty good in the right circumstances', but that the students had not been fully able to transfer their skills to other situations. Although the training programme had focused on these skills, they remained unconsolidated. The most positive outcome of the training for this teacher at this stage was that the students were able to develop these skills in an atmosphere of safety and trust, 'they know that in circle time they are going to be given a chance to say what they want, and nobody is going to criticize them for saying what they want.'

By the final interviews it was clear that the students in this school had had opportunities to practise and assimilate their skills through peer mediation, and that they had begun to transfer them to other situations. One of the teachers of the classes who had been part of the programme felt that her students had assimilated conflict-resolution skills:

They're quite good at it without realising what they're doing. Because of the mediation course they went on last year, they know that they're helping people to solve problems, but I don't think they realise quite how difficult their job is and how well they do it … they'll sit there and they'll listen. Whereas I think an adult is always prone to say something, they can sit back and listen. I think probably they're better at it than some of us.

According to this class teacher at this time, circle time was ongoing, with her students using it to talk about issues that concerned them:

They really enjoy circle time … we do a range of things from games to discussing quite important issues to them. It's nice that they want to do it. It's supposed to be for an hour, but it's usually stretched. They really like it and it's one of the few times when they will sit still for a length of time.

The success of these circle-time sessions appears to be related to the students feeling ownership. This teacher felt that these techniques had particularly helped with the inclusion of a child with social emotional and behavioural difficulties:

I have a young chap in my class who's got a history of having a very short fuse, and I have had a lot of negative feed-back from home. We've worked very hard with him this year, and now he is able to vocalise his feelings … without resorting to thumping people, which is what he was doing last year. I mean, even (the headteacher) has noticed that. He sat down and talked through an incident with her last week, whereas last year that wouldn't have happened. It would have been a case of somebody coming in crying. Now he's talking through it and explaining why he is unhappy. One of the children concerned said 'let's discuss it' and we had a circle time, an impromptu one really, just because they wanted to do it that way. He felt comfortable with the perimeters of the circle time situation.

The time that this teacher had invested in developing these skills, values and attitudes had clearly paid off, particularly for this young person with SEBD. Another teacher of a parallel class felt that, by the end of the full programme, 'There are very few occasions when we have any clashes or anything disruptive.' She was able to recall 'all sorts of occasions' when the students had worked together cooperatively: 'a lot of art work they've worked on together, science activities as well. I think they're pretty good with that – it shows in many ways.' This teacher also recalled a situation in which a silver bracelet had gone missing during a physical education (PE) lesson. The bracelet had been replaced by the child who had taken it after a circle time session in which all children had been able to express their disappointment that the incident had taken place:

> I think that this is what's really accentuated it for me. This would have been a very difficult incident to sort out, especially the day after, and it had to be handled carefully. I think that the fact that all children witnessed and heard what everybody else felt and were able to say what should happen affected the child who took it. We still don't know to this day who took it, but it really was a most magnificent breakthrough to get it back and to have sorted it out in this way.

She went on to reflect on the ways in which student-centred discipline had, 'become sort of ingrained in the class'. She identified, 'a level of maturity that has come out over the months because of what we've been doing ...' She clearly saw the peer mediation programme as key to these successful outcomes, stating that this maturity was, 'not apparent beforehand'.

The second and third interviews with the teachers of the two classes who had participated in the peer mediation training programme only in School Two revealed that the students' awareness of conflict resolution techniques had generally improved, but that their ability to act on their awareness was not always evident. One of the class teachers commented that fighting was still occurring, and, 'once they have let loose their views, they seem to want to sort it out afterwards, when they've calmed down.' This teacher also felt that the students' ability to express their feelings and needs had largely not progressed beyond their need for teacher support, 'we do a lot of talking with the children, but that would be very much with an adult mediator. They don't automatically try to resolve things themselves.' This is not surprising, given the fact that no peer mediation service was established in this school!

In School Two, any improvements in students' skills were not sustained. One of the class teachers commented that although the students' cooperation skills and group-work had improved, 'The wrong thing will be said and it's gone, which is a shame. It's like sitting on a time bomb.' A comment from a class teacher during the final interview reveals the frustration that they were feeling (in marked contrast to the teachers in School One) and, possibly, the consequences of not implementing the full peer mediation programme:

> Oh dear, we always plug and plug away at co-operating with each other, getting on together. If you can't get on, if you can't say a good thing, there's no need to say a bad thing. I keep saying to them, I'm not going to give up, come July we'll still be saying it to you. We may

or may not have got anywhere ... it might work for a week or two weeks, and then have to be reinstalled, but we keep going.

As in School Two, it emerged during the second and third interviews with the class teachers in School Three that the students' awareness of conflict resolution techniques had generally improved but that their ability to act on their awareness was not always in evidence. During the second interview, one of the teachers said of her class, 'they are aware of the strategies and the skills (of conflict resolution) but they don't always employ them ... they probably need more practice, more encouragement to do it.' Another teacher in this school at this time said that any improvements in her students' ability to affirm each other were not sustained:

> That again varies, depending on what's been going on in the school, who they've had, if they've been disrupted. If it's just after a holiday, then they're not very good at it, and on a Monday they can sometimes be a bit off. The middle of the week is fine, the end of the week is fine.

Likewise, their listening skills were not sustained. The students were less able to listen to each other in a supportive way outside of the 'life skills' lessons in which the peer mediation training took place, 'in the lessons we've done they're very good, they will listen and they will give support, but if they don't think it's a specific lesson, they're not necessarily as good.' During the final interviews one of the class teachers in this school stated that, 'they know they should be co-operating, but sometimes they are not transferring it' and the other teacher gives an example of how these skills have still not been consolidated:

> We did outdoor and adventure PE, and they loved that. They were very good at working as a team ... until it came to – if you had points for anything, it was always somebody else's fault they hadn't got as many, or they cheated, or whatever. Actually playing the game, no problem, so you'd be feeling 'Oh, this lesson's gone really well, aren't they marvellous', then some stupid little thing would happen and you'd be thinking 'Oh, crumbs!'

Conclusion

Student-centred behaviour management, and peer mediation in particular, supports inclusion by involving all students in taking responsibility for the resolution of conflict in school. Based on humanistic principles, it provides an environment in which students can review the effects of their behaviour while feeling valued and accepted by their teacher and peers. It focuses on the development of an internalized moral code and set of behavioural norms, and therefore encourages an internal locus of control. It requires students to have acquired the necessary social cognitive skills to engage in the process of reviewing behaviour, and it requires teachers to provide students with the psychological space to develop self-discipline as opposed to imposed discipline. More directive behaviour management, such as authoritarian and behaviourist methods, may well be necessary at times to maintain student safety, but the adverse effects of punishment, and the over-reliance on teacher control, result in students who have little emotional investment in contributing to a classroom culture in which peer mediation will thrive. The research into peer mediation reviewed here suggested that peer mediation training programmes lead only to a partial acquisition of skills, which need to be consolidated in real situations. Where this consolidation does occur, peer mediation is shown to be a powerful tool for behaviour management and inclusion of students experiencing SEBD. Failure to progress to the full implementation of peer mediation is associated with teachers remaining in control of the management of behaviour in school, and an abdication of responsibility on the part of students, who remain immature in attitude and at times difficult to control.

5 Empowerment, the voice of the child, and peer mediation

Introduction

Student voice is concerned with how students express their interests, perspectives and values through interactions with others in a variety of arenas where they have differing degrees of control. Empowerment within a school context refers to the degree to which students feel that they are able to influence their school environment, and the degree to which they feel consulted and enabled to bring about positive change. This chapter reviews how children's voices are restricted by 'child panic' and dual attitudes towards childhood, with children seen as both in need of protection and as aggressors from whom adults need to be protected. It is argued more generally that a command-and-control culture within the education sector as a whole militates against processes of consultation, whether these processes involve students or teachers. This chapter will build on the previous three by outlining some benefits and challenges of engaging with the voice of the child, and by giving examples of the ways in which peer mediation can contribute. It will draw on ideas expounded in Chapter Two on empowering and communitarian approaches to the resolution of conflict, ideas from Chapter Three on the role of citizenship education in engaging with young people's perspectives, and ideas from Chapter Four on collaborative approaches to developing student-centred discipline in schools. Circle time is reviewed here, with Taylor's (2003) research used to provide examples of the ways in which some teachers find it hard to let go of power and control, even during an activity that is supposed to be empowering for students. Cremin's (2001) research is revisited to explore similar themes, and research by Sellman (2002) and Bickmore (2001) explores the values and practices that underpin the successful implementation of peer mediation. In considering how schools take account of student voices, it is useful to begin with consideration of how children's voices are heard more generally in society.

The voice of the child

The notion of the voice of the child is grounded in a 'new sociology of childhood' (James et al., 2005), which sees childhood as a social construction and calls for children to be 'treated as a minority, and defined as a disadvantaged, excluded group who deserve greater social, political and economic rights' (Brooks, 2006). These perspectives have grown in an era marked by both a 'sustained assault on childhood' (adult incursions into children's spaces) and 'a concern for children' (attempts to keep children safe from harmful adult influences) (Brooks, 2006: 3). James et al. talk about the new sociology of childhood in terms of a 'rise of childhood agency', the 'transition from the child as an instance of a category to the recognition of children as particular persons' and a 'new paradigm' of children as 'social actors shaping as well as shaped by their circumstances' (James et al., 2005: 6). The UK's ratification of the UN convention on the Rights of the Child in 1990, the Children Acts (1989, 2004), the UK government's Every Child Matters reform programme, and the appointment of the first Children's Commissioner for England in 2005 (following appointments in Wales and Scotland) are all signs that the momentum for taking account of children's perspectives is growing.

There is, however, a serious and unhelpful split in the way that childhood is viewed. This split is not new and can be characterized as a dichotomy between two dominant images of childhood: the one emphasizing 'the natural wildness of children'; and the other 'their natural innocence' (Ruddock and Flutter, 2004: 3). The first image of the wildness of childhood can be traced back to the growing influence of Christianity in the seventeenth century (Ariès, 1962). The belief that all infants were burdened with original sin led to a view of childhood as a moral and spiritual preparation for a more pious adult life. The enlightenment replaced religion with reason but the concepts remained the same. Locke argued that the child is a blank slate, and that teachers should prepare children for a life of enlightened rationality. The contrasting image of the innocence of childhood can be traced back to Rousseau, the eighteenth-century French philosopher who countered that goodness is contained in the natural state of childhood, and that children should be free to explore the world around them, nurtured by a responsive teacher. These ideas were celebrated and developed by Romantic writers such as Blake and Wordsworth in the late eighteenth and early nineteenth centuries.

The same dichotomy can be seen in the twentieth century. Hardyman (cited in Brooks, 2006) points out that parents in the early part of the twentieth century were advised to maintain strict routines for feeding and sleeping, and to keep indulgencies to a minimum. This, she argues, suited a world where war dominated public consciousness. After the Second World War, however, parents reacted against the regimes of fascism and totalitarianism by rearing children who would be free thinkers. This was developed further in the 1960s revolution through exhortations for parents to enjoy their children and to trust their own instincts.

The wild/innocent dichotomy of childhood is as confused and para-doxical as ever in the early part of the twenty-first century, with both images coexisting in the public consciousness. Brooks (2006) notes that concern about the vulnerability of some children has now been traduced by an all-pervading child-panic. She characterizes the split thus: 'Our children are in danger, preyed upon by paedophiles, corrupted by commerce, traumatised by testing. Our children are dangerous: malevolent beneath hooded tops, chaotic in the classroom, bestial in the bedroom' (Brooks, 2006: 16).

These divided views on childhood can be unhelpful when they lead to confused or ineffective action to improve children's lives. Even the notion of children's rights is sometimes greeted with hostility in a political climate where young people are often marginalized for their lack of respect for the rights of others or adult authority. Some adult fears relate to discombobula-tion at the shape of the modern world, and nostalgia for a time before mobile phones and breast implants and 24-hour advertising (Brookes, 2006). They respond by trying to create a safe and separate space for childhood. But can young people shoulder the burden of adult loss? If they are born into an environment of conspicuous consumption, sexual saturation and violence, then perhaps 'adults need to equip them with the tools to cope with this rather than perpetuate the fantasy that it is possible to shelter them from it entirely' (Ibid: 333). In this, education (and citizenship education in parti-cular) is key.

The voice of the child in educational settings

The effects of these divided views on childhood, so much in evidence in the media and society at large, are intensified in educational settings. Ruddock and Flutter (2004: 1) note that, 'out of school many young people find themselves involved in complex relationships and situations, and carry tough responsibilities', but that 'in contrast, the structures of secondary schooling offer, on the whole, less responsibility and autonomy than many young people are accustomed to...' This provides schools with a real challenge, especially when the curriculum can seem outdated and stultified to some young people, 'compared with TV and soaps and youth magazines, there are fewer occasions when anxieties and aspirations can be opened up and explored' (Ruddock and Flutter, 2004: 1). If these dilemmas are not addressed in consultation with young people, then it is hard to see how progress can be made towards insuring that schools meet their needs. Apple (1995) whose ideas on the all-pervasiveness of neoliberalism have been explored in some depth in Chapter Three recognizes that there is a need to subvert and disrupt dominant discourses and practices in schools through engaging with diverse voices, especially marginalized voices, and creating culture and practice that takes account of human need at a more localized level:

> Relations of dominance, then, and of necessity struggles against them, are not theoretical abstractions, somewhere out there in an ethereal sphere unconnected to daily life. Rather, they are based on and built out of an entire network of daily social and cultural relations and practices. Dominance depends on both leadership and legitimation. It is not simply an imposition ...
>
> (Apple, 1995: xv)

To this end, Ruddock and Flutter (2004) outline five 'advocacies' for engaging with the voice of the child in schools. These are: the importance of helping students to develop their identities and individual voices; the need for young people to be able to 'speak out' about matters that concern them; a recognition that in the task of change, students are the 'expert witnesses'; the need for policy makers and schools to understand and respect the world of young people; and the importance of preparing young people to be citizens in a democratic society (Ruddock and Flutter, 2004: 101).

Huddleston and Rowe (2003: 122) make some recommendations for how schools might address the need to engage with student voice at classroom level. They stress the importance of teacher skill and patience in working to create an atmosphere 'in which all students feel they have something to contribute and are able to express themselves freely'. They outline the principles of creating such an atmosphere. Teachers should choose limited, achievable goals, intersperse discussion with other activities, establish ground rules, give everyone something to say and pay attention to classroom layout. Teachers should also build in time for debriefing on the processes involved, not just the outcomes, and train young people in generic skills of participating in a public space. They should provide a role model for how to engage in discussion, while managing and facilitating the discussion of others.

Huddleston and Kerr (2006: 84) argue that students should be consulted about school issues because 'they have a right to be involved in decisions that affect them; it is an important opportunity for citizenship learning; and it improves relationships and promotes dialogue in school.' They point out that taking on positions of responsibility helps students to see themselves as active members of a community, grow in confidence and maturity, acquire new skills, knowledge and understanding, and prepare for a world beyond school. For this to happen, students need to be fully briefed about their responsibilities, given support and training, and to have opportunities to discuss their experiences and reflect on them in their personal portfolio and/or progress file. They give the 'Students-as-Researchers' movement as an example of one of the most significant student participation developments in recent years, 'because of its potential to re-draw organisational lines of responsibility and accountability in school' (Huddleston and Kerr, 2006: 94). Hastingsbury Upper School in Bedford was one of the first schools in England to set up a 'Students-as-Researchers' group. The group developed as a subcommittee of the student council. The students involved collected and analysed information and evidence on specific school issues and reported their findings to students and staff.

In 2004, Hannam, in association with Community Service Volunteers, carried out a study investigating young people's views on consultation and the methods they found to be preferable. The main focus of the data collection was on four schools known to have active and effective school student councils. These school councils had already engaged in research into whole-school issues. They also had well-established peer mentoring programmes with a strong element of student leadership. One day was spent in each school. Thirty-five students at key stage two (seven-to-11-year-olds) including the entire school council, were interviewed at a primary school. Eighteen students from key stages two and three (nine-to-13-year-olds) were interviewed at a middle school. Twenty-four students from key stages three and four (13-to-16-year-olds) and six post-16 students were interviewed at two upper schools. Between them these schools provided interview opportunities with students from a full range of social and ethnic backgrounds and prior academic attainment, including those at risk of alienation and disengagement. Students in these listening schools were willing to 'give it a try', participate and communicate their ideas to a wide range of audiences, including national government. They were motivated to share their perceptions in order to benefit themselves and other students. They had some confidence that such an exercise would be worthwhile, although there was also scepticism about the extent to which their ideas would be acted upon. Individual students in these schools believed that they could enhance the quality of information provided by young people through their participation in the consultation process. They felt that they were better placed than adults to reach out to peers who were reluctant to be drawn into consultative processes and had ideas about how these peers could be involved. In fact, they doubted that any consultation project that failed to listen to the full spectrum of student voice could ever be successful.

It is noteworthy that these students recognized both the vital importance of engaging with the full spectrum of student voice and the challenges that this presents for adults charged with responding to what students have said. Ruddock and Flutter (2004: 115) warn that the task of 'teaching democracy' in schools is a 'considerable challenge' and quote Cook-Sather (2002: 3) who notes that 'authorising students' perspectives' involves changes 'in mindset' as well as 'changes in the structure of educational relationships'. Quoting Davie and Galloway (1996), Hancock and Mansfield (2002) suggest that, although the idea that teachers should consult children in order to be better informed professionals has been increasingly recognized, education lags behind some other child services in terms of heeding what children have to say. They argue that despite a professional rhetoric about the importance of consulting with children, there is reason to think that many teachers continue to disregard children's views in their day-to-day practice. Their study, on which these conclusions are based, involved 48 children talking about their experiences of the literacy hour (a national strategy aimed at raising children's achievement). It found that children raised important theoretical and practical issues that required attention, but that, 'at a time when the primary school curriculum is increasingly defined by those outside the classroom, children are at risk of not being seriously considered or consulted' (Hancock and Mansfield, 2002: 197). They go on to suggest that an educational climate which disempowers teachers is also likely to disempower children, 'Within a command and control structure, teachers are likely to command children in the way they themselves are being commanded' (Hancock and Mansfield, 2002: 185).

Teachers may feel that they are consulting with their students, even when their actions suggest otherwise. This dichotomy may well be linked with the split in attitudes towards childhood outlined earlier in the chapter, and with the all-pervasiveness of neoliberalism outlined earlier in the book. Differing and contradictory discourses on education and childhood play out in teachers' minds and actions in ways that are complex and hard to trace back. Pollard and Triggs (2000) found that although teachers in their study thought that they placed a fairly high priority on developing autonomy, confidence and independence in learning, their students' experience was of little free choice and 'strong and increasing teacher control' (Triggs, 2000: 84).

In a systematic review of the impact of citizenship education on the provision of schooling, Deakin Crick et al. found (2004) that teachers may need to 'let go of control' in order to listen effectively to the voices of their students, and that they may require support to develop appropriate professional skills to do this. They suggest that strategies for bringing about consensual change have to be developed in educational leaders, and that schools often restrict participation by students in shaping institutional practices while expecting them to adhere to those practices. All of this is counterproductive to the core messages of citizenship education, which requires a coherent whole-school strategy, including a community-owned values framework. Their recommendations for policy and practice for effective citizenship education include the need for school-based decision making, an enhanced culture of professional autonomy amongst teachers, and a learner-centred approach to teaching and learning in schools. They stress the importance of national educational policy that encourages diversity rather than uniformity, and responsiveness to local needs.

A case in point is research carried out amongst 60 disaffected students in Lancashire, UK, to identify the reasons behind their disaffection and educational exclusion (Riley and Rustique-Forrester, 2002). As well as engaging with the voices of the young people themselves, the authors audited a range of projects aimed at reducing disaffection, and interviewed both school-based and non-school-based professionals, and parents. Although the research unearthed frustration and mistrust, it also revealed a communality of perceptions about what needs to change. Students in schools, and adults with a wide variety of roles, all agreed that the key to change lies in rethinking the nature of teaching and learning. There was agreement that interplay between teachers and students was extremely important, and that the solutions to the many problems faced by these communities lie within their own grasp. All agreed that headteachers and teachers have too little time for reflection and that they are forced to respond to competing external and internal demands. All wanted teachers to have time and space to work with individual students and more professional development opportunities. A blueprint for change was put to 80 secondary headteachers at a conference in Lancashire, and was enthusiastically seen as relevant and applicable. There were reservations, however, about the extent to which the changes could be made. The frustration of all was expressed in the words of one headteacher, 'I've got to call the Rottweillers off. I've really got to pull back and stop pushing my teachers just to achieve the targets. We've got to start talking about children and about learning' (Riley and Rustique-Forrester, 2002: 69).

In a climate where (despite political rhetoric) teachers and headteachers are more accountable to central government than to their local communities, it is difficult to imagine how strategies to engage with student voice can be fully implemented. Democratic governments, of course, function only with a mandate from the electorate and blame for difficulties in engaging with student voice cannot be left solely at the government's door. The origins of these difficulties can also be traced back to flawed and contradictory attitudes towards childhood and education residing within the public consciousness. Ruddock and Flutter (2004) summarize these issues well, and present a series of questions that relate to ongoing tensions between a view of schooling that is past-orientated, and a view that is future-orientated:

> Are our images of the students we want in school over-influenced by values from the past? Should we instead be working back from the virtues and capacities we want to see in post-school-age citizens? Are the virtues we seek in students ones that will make for a quiet life in school and classroom, but have a limited shelf-life beyond school? Do we have a basic set of values about humankind that we are

> looking to distil? Are we looking for study skills or coping skills – and as preparation for life and lifelong learning or just the exams?
>
> (Ruddock and Flutter, 2004: 132)

It seems that, until adults are able to properly examine the roots of 'child panic', neoliberalism and neoconservatism in schools, the student voice project could be severely limited before it has had a chance to bear fruit.

Peer mediation and the voice of the child

This next section will explore some of the issues highlighted above through concrete examples of implementing peer mediation and circle time in schools. Circle time is a focus here as it shares peer mediation's grounding in student voice and humanistic psychology, and as it is often used as a basis for training and supporting peer mediators in schools. The section will begin by focusing on a review of circle time carried out by Taylor (2003) and will continue by reporting in some detail on research into the implementation of peer mediation in primary schools in the UK and Canada (Cremin, 2001; Bickmore, 2001).

Circle time was first named and formalized as an approach by Ballard (1982) in the US. He encouraged students to use circle time to listen supportively to each other, and to develop social skills and a more positive self-concept. Ballard based circle time on the principles of humanistic therapy, creating a safe environment in which students felt valued, listened to and supported. He encouraged self-expression (in particular the expression of emotions) and creative problem solving. In the UK, circle time has been developed and extended in the past few decades to an extent where it is rare to hear of a school that does not use circle time in some way. Stacey and Robinson (1997) describe circle time as a time when students sit in a circle, and take it in turns to speak (a go-round) using a talking object. Only the person holding the object is allowed to talk, and anything that anyone says is treated with respect (no put downs). Cooperative games are often played, and it is a time for fun, inclusion and sharing. Goldthorpe (1998) summarizes the approach used by Jenny Mosley as following a series of stages. These are an opening game, raising an issue, open forum, celebrating success and an ending ritual. To set the agenda for the open forum, a 'go-round' can be used to gather information about how everyone feels (for example 'When people leave me out of games I feel . . .'). The open forum can be used by the group to set some targets for addressing the issue (for example 'To stop people feeling lonely at playtime I will . . .'). This follows the same format as mediation and is based on the same non-directive principles of inclusion and acceptance.

Stacey (2001) lists some of the benefits of circle time amongst children in

Stockport, as reported by headteachers as: improved behaviour, for example turn taking; improved speaking and listening skills; improved concentration; more positive peer relationships; improved conflict resolution skills; greater emotional development; raised self-esteem; improved confidence; and a stronger group identity. Goldthorpe (1998) lists some benefits reported by schools as: improved team-work amongst staff, children and helpers; a positive caring atmosphere in school; improved relationships between teachers and their classes; raised self-esteem; children who are more responsible for their own behaviour; improved tolerance and support of peers; the creation of time and space for reflection and problem solving in a positive non-threatening atmosphere; and improved speaking and listening skills.

Despite its success, circle time is an example of an initiative which has grown informally from school to school, without teachers necessarily undertaking professional development, or understanding theoretical underpinnings. Taylor (2003) makes reference to confusion between pedagogic and psychological approaches to circle time. Much of the poor practice that is described in Taylor's report (and there is some good practice) seems to be a direct result of this confusion. The examples that follow illustrate how an approach that is supposed to give students the opportunity to find their 'voice' can revert back to a means of directing learning, and controlling students' behaviour.

Taylor's report is based on telephone and face-to-face interviews with circle time trainers, headteachers from 57 schools (or their circle time coordinators) and students in 14 case-study schools. Observations of circle-time sessions also occurred in these case-study schools. Key findings centre around professional, pedagogical and practice issues, and around concerns relating to school ethos, ethics and matching aims with outcomes.

Taylor (2003: 56) describes how in School B the three main rules of circle time are described by a class teacher, 'don't interrupt, sit as straight as possible, and don't get upset.' Apart from the number of rules (three) there is little relation here between what the teacher is asking of the children and the rules for circle time advocated by the proponents of circle time. There is clear confusion here between the need for rules to create a safe environment for sharing and a teacher's desire to maintain classroom control. Presumably, a child who is being ridiculed in the circle would have very little redress unless the person who was ridiculing them was not sitting up straight! The child is barred from protecting himself/herself (don't interrupt) and from showing any feeling (don't get upset). This is the opposite of what circle time is supposed to achieve. Likewise two year-four girls describe an incident when a boy whom they characterize as 'scared of school' did circle time on his first day in his new class in his new school:

> When it got to him he said 'I don't want to do it,' and the teacher
> said 'You are only allowed one pass,' cos he passed the second time
> and then he started crying and he kept shouting at the teacher ... So
> he had to go in the corner and wasn't allowed to join in the Circle
> Time.
>
> (Taylor, 2003: 119)

The playing of parachute games in School K is described (Taylor, 2003: 71). The playing of the game: 'required a lot of direction and organisation from the teacher,' but, 'did not require any talking from the students.' A small disruption led the teacher to ask, 'What do you do if I blow the whistle?' The students replied in chorus, 'Stop.' Valuable lessons in working as a team, and overcoming difficulties are therefore lost as the teacher takes charge and becomes overly controlling. Somehow the point is lost that the value of parachute games lies not in the students managing to make the perfect dome, but in the process of cooperation and teamwork. The real learning comes from overcoming some of the challenges that teams face as they struggle to achieve something as group. The young people are robbed of a valuable learning opportunity if their thinking is done for them by their teacher.

In some of the sessions described, the teachers are clear from the outset what they want the students to do and say. In School E, a teacher describes how, 'Setting up the circle time is very important so that the students understand the types of things I am trying to get them to do ...' (Taylor, 2003: 65). The circle time session run by this teacher is based on the assumption that circle time should teach some key predetermined learning objectives. For example, to elicit responses to the question of what you should do if you see someone being picked on, she avoids using a go-round (which would have involved all 'voices' in the class) and asks for hands up. She therefore does not give everyone the opportunity to respond and endorses some of the contributions but not others. The children may just as well have been sitting at tables for this – the circle is redundant. In another school a teacher asks a question during a circle time, 'Is it a good idea for you to go and punch someone?' (Taylor, 2003: 70). In School K, the teacher is described using 'guess what is on my mind' techniques, asking a child how a small soft ball might make someone feel 'warm and fuzzy' (Taylor, 2003: 58). The child (perhaps unsurprisingly) fails to respond, at which point the teacher gives an example which the child agrees with.

The children in some of the interviews are clear about the real power dynamics in their circle time sessions, despite the rhetoric of equality. In School K, a year-four girl talks about problem solving in circle time to 'sort out' people who have been 'naughty' (Taylor, 2003: 64). She says that the teacher, 'would listen to you, and she would get the person in that class to come over and say sorry.' Presumably this is independent of whether the 'naughty' person actually did feel sorry or understood how his/her actions had affected another person. The students in School B describe how their teacher maintains her ability to make judgements about their contributions in circle time, 'If they don't agree then they wait their turn and then start lecturing you' (Taylor, 2003: 127). Some students felt silenced or controlled in circle time. Taylor gives an example of a year-four girl in School L expressing her frustration that she had brought two Greek dolls in from her collection, but had not been allowed to show or talk about them (Taylor, 2003: 126). Taylor points out that, 'students reinforced our perception that few teachers asked them what they liked or didn't like about circle time.' In School K a year-four girl describes how she made something up in the 'Child of the Day' activity as she was under pressure to say something positive about a child she did not like and did not want to appear 'bad tempered' (Taylor, 2003: 63).

It can certainly be argued that skills-building and clear learning objectives for circle time are a good idea, but it is harder to argue for these things when the result is that students are disempowered in the one area of school life where they could be free to explore issues and concerns that are meaningful to them, and to collaborate to find their own solutions to their own problems. This is against the principles of humanistic education and student 'voice'. An example from School F (Taylor, 2003: 57) bears more detailed analysis in order to illustrate this point. At the end of the summer term, when year-two children were expressing fear about changing classes, the teacher directed them to close their eyes and to remember their feelings the previous year when they had started their new class. She then got them to speak about what they had particularly enjoyed during the previous school year. In this way she attempted to allay their fears by teaching them that they had already coped with change with positive results, and would thus be able to cope with any changes in the future. She concluded the session by complimenting the class, saying, 'I've enjoyed teaching such a grown-up sensible class. I've been able to write some lovely reports about everyone, and you are all hard-working.' This approach appears to be drawing from cognitive psychology, which suggests that a therapist (teacher?) can reduce fear and negative feelings through providing information and rational arguments in a calm atmosphere.

Humanistic psychology, and therefore humanistic education, holds that the individual grows and learns to cope with fears and negative emotions though expressing them in an environment where there is empathy, unconditional positive regard, and genuineness on the part of the therapist or teacher (Rogers and Freiberg, 1994). The role of the teacher in this situation is purely facilitative. Fundamental to humanistic education is the teacher's non-directive and non-judgemental role, and willingness to engage with the voice of the child. The teacher in the above example, with no doubt the very best of intentions, was being both directive and judgemental and was ignoring children's voices. She was using a pedagogical approach to teach the children that their fears are ungrounded, and she was reminding them, albeit in a positive way, that as their teacher she is making judgements about them all the time. A teacher using a humanistic approach in this same situation would have given the children time to express their feelings of trepidation. She would then have reflected these feelings back to them in a warm and supportive way before asking them to share with each other any suggestions for how these fears might best be dealt with. This has the advantage over the methods used by the teacher in School F that the children remain in control over the whole process. Not only does this impact on their self-confidence, reminding them that, with support, they are best placed to resolve their own difficulties, but it also has the advantage that any solutions that the children come up with (invite people from your class to your house the day before you start back, walk to school with a friend, show your mum around you new classroom) come from the needs and perspectives of a six- or seven-year-old. Are they not better placed to support each other with ideas for resolving difficulties than even well-intentioned adults?

Turning now to research into the implementation of peer mediation in three primary schools reported in Chapter Three and Four (Cremin, 2001), it is clear, once more, that a humanistically orientated ethos and a willingness to engage with the student voice is key to the success of peer mediation. During the interviews that were carried out as part of the research programme, the headteacher and teachers in School One showed themselves to be genuinely interested in the feelings, experiences and perspectives of the young people in their charge, and able to interact with them in ways that allowed reciprocity, shared decision making, and trust. During the final interview with the peer mediation coordinator in this school, the value that the school placed on student voice became apparent:

> I think some of the children feel like they have quite a lot of control, just because of some things that have happened over the year ... where they have been asked about what they'd like or what the problems are, and people like the deputy headteacher have actually listened, and changes have happened in school. Now if you ask some of those children what they'll miss most, or what they think will happen when they leave the school, they say things like: 'Well I hope the dinner-time rota doesn't go just because we've gone', because they feel that they've set that up. Quite a few of them feel like that.

The personal and social skills needed for these processes were highly valued, and consistently taught. The students in School One enjoyed using their skills during circle time, and during peer mediation, with the result that they felt ownership over the process of the resolution of student conflicts in school.

These outcomes appeared to be linked with school ethos, which the headteacher of School One summarized in her first interview, 'The ethos of this school is already one of listening to children, valuing children. That means not blaming the child when it is the ineffectiveness of the curriculum or model that's at fault.' She was keen to use peer mediation as a means of embedding ethos into practice, and gave an example of the kinds of adult intervention that she wanted to discourage through this new intervention:

> Sometimes adults arrive at the wrong conclusion because they use a heavy hand, or because the authoritarian role they have, as deputy or head, results in the children parroting the words they think the adult wants to hear, rather than resolving the problem. You send them away having said the right things and having assumed the right body-posture, and they go out and do exactly the same thing again because, actually, you haven't reached them on the right note.

During a second interview, when the peer mediation skills training was complete (but the actual service itself had not yet been set up) this head-teacher noted that she was already seeing fewer aggressive disputes coming as far as her office door. She paraphrased what she felt most students believed: 'I can confidently engage in conversations because I think you want to listen to what I've got to say, and I expect that if I am courteous, and I use people's names, and I wait my turn, I expect what I have to say to be valued, because I am a member of the school, the family.' In this, she reaffirmed the link between student voice and effective conflict resolution in her school. By the final interview, when peer mediation was up and running, the headteacher was talking about 'Road to Damascus stuff'. She summarized the ways in which she felt progress had been made:

> They (students) are becoming very skilled at saying, 'Oh, I can see why you thought that.' They are becoming faster at seeing points at which they could have intervened or could have changed the out-come ... I have been impressed with two groups of girls recently ... at the maturity of their interpretation of their own behaviour, and I'm sure that that's because they've got into a more reflective habit.

This headteacher also made it clear in her final interview that circle time was a key strategy for engaging with student voice, and that it was being used by the teachers in her school in a humanistic way. She gave an example of what had happened when an educational psychologist went into a circle-time lesson to observe a child, 'He brought himself out of the class after 30 minutes because he was moved to the point of tears by the conduct of circle time and the quite deep-seated feelings the children felt able to express in the classroom.'

She noted that this level of support for circle time had not been in evidence from the start, but was quickly adopted by teachers as they saw the benefits:

> Children enjoy it so much, and I think that comes through quite a lot in every classroom now. It's a forum for them to be heard. I think the fact that it has very clear rules helps, and I think it's making a good contribution to work in general. We've used it as part of English, as part of speaking and listening, but I think that it goes a lot further, a lot deeper than anything, any curriculum, and school curriculum, could provide for a child.

The ethos in Schools Two and Three did not appear to be humanistically orientated and there was less of an emphasis on engaging with student voice. In both schools, the headteachers and teachers felt that direct adult control was necessary to retain order and a positive learning environment in school. This need for control appeared to be based on an underlying belief that students were not to be trusted and attempts at engaging with student voice were limited. Rogers and Freiberg (1994) have said of this, 'The freedom to learn requires a special understanding of what it takes to establish an open learning environment. Granting freedom is not a method, it's a philosophy. Unless you really believe that students can be trusted with responsibility, you won't be successful.' Perhaps this is why the full peer mediation programme was not implemented in Schools Two and Three, with a resulting lack of change in levels of bullying.

An illustration of this lack of engagement with student voice can be seen in some of the things that the teachers in School Three said during their interviews. In response to a question about student feelings of empowerment, one of the teachers in this school noted:

> Inside the classroom they have to adhere to quite strict rules and regulations, I try to make them as independent as I can, but they do have to do the work in order for me to give it to them ... and they have to stay in their seats. It's a very controlled environment, very imposed discipline, but at the same time I think they feel that they are fairly treated ...

Another teacher in this school, interviewed at the same time, stated that, 'I would say that they have very little control when I am there, but they certainly have a great deal of control when I am not there, shall we say?' This teacher's ironic, 'shall we say?' was taken to convey that she felt that her students used control destructively when she was not there to supervise them. She later went on to clarify that she felt that students manipulated situations where they were given freedom.

This suggests shared attitudes amongst these teachers in this school that students couldn't be trusted with control over their environment, unless it was in ways that had been negotiated with the teacher. Within such a tight structure of teacher-centred power and control it is hard to see how it would have been possible to engage in a genuine way with the voice of the child, or to implement an initiative such as peer mediation, which relies on students being trained and supported to take responsible action on behalf of peers, without direct adult supervision. In these circumstances, students are denied opportunities for learning to use power and control responsibly in the classroom and playground. They are denied opportunities for developing creative problem-solving skills in real-life situations, and are kept in a relatively powerless position where pleasing the teacher is a precondition to receiving limited choice.

The headteacher of this school (School Three) revealed certain erroneous assumptions about peer mediation in her first and second interviews (a third interview was not possible). During the initial interview, she made links between what she saw as the 'moral' element of peer mediation, and the Christian values within her school:

> We do spend a lot of time on the catholicity of the school ... I just think it (peer mediation) is another tool, or implement, or skill, that we'll have in *making* the children love and care for each other, which we continually preach to them in assemblies about ... It's something that, whilst we haven't called it what you're calling it, in a general way we might well have been doing it.

The use of the word 'making' (italicized above for emphasis) is perhaps key here. The headteacher of School Three was concerned with imparting the values and attitudes of Catholicism onto her students, in contrast with the headteacher in School One who was concerned from the outset with using peer mediation as a vehicle for hearing the student voice in as authentic a way as possible. One leadership stance involved the headteacher as 'transmitter'; the other involved the headteacher as 'receptor'. The headteacher in School Three equates preaching in assembly with the techniques and strategies of peer mediation. Indeed, throughout both interviews, the headteacher did not at any time refer to enskilling or empowering students. When asked during the first interview what she would like to see coming out of the peer mediation programme, her desired outcomes mainly involved adult power and control. The first concerned adults being directive (but not punitive) with students: 'There are occasions when we (the teachers) could say, "This is the way of resolving it", rather than somebody just being chastened verbally.' The second concerned using peer mediation to 'smooth the rough edges of the school'. On the one hand these rough edges were described as 'their relationships with each other', and on the other they were described as 'the mode of entry in and out of assembly'.

These leadership styles appeared to have been key in the success, or otherwise, of peer mediation in these schools. It is interesting to reflect on this in the light of discussion earlier in the chapter about the values and beliefs surrounding the notion of childhood. The dichotomy of the natural wildness of children, and their natural innocence, can be seen in the differing values and beliefs of these two headteachers. The head in School One wanted to draw out their natural goodness; the head in School Three wanted to tame their natural wildness. The fact that the latter school is grounded strongly in Catholicism may be significant here.

The headteacher in School Two was different again. She certainly had the desire to engage with student voice and to empower her students to a greater degree, but she underestimated the degree of change that needed to take place within the school in order for this to happen. During her first interview, this headteacher focused on anecdotes, and on the 'truisms' that she liked to share with children during assemblies and her walks around school, rather than on analysis of what she wanted to change through this intervention, or on how she might ensure the success of the intervention. It became clear during the final interview with the headteacher that peer mediation in this school had not reached a successful conclusion because teachers had not engaged with a process of reviewing school culture and ethos. The head regretted that students who had been trained as peer mediators, 'were led to believe ... that peer mediation was the answer to disputes. They have now found through experience that a dispute is solved the way it was always solved ... by confrontation.'

In a similar way to the other two schools, there were strong parallels in School Two between the values and attitudes expressed by teachers in their interviews, and those expressed by the headteacher. The teachers in School Two made it clear throughout that the main strategies used to combat bullying were structure and control. One of the teachers stated that there was not much bullying in the classroom because 'the day is very structured', and the other that there was not much bullying in the classroom because 'I feel that I keep quite tight control of the children.' She extended this to lunchtime by saying that there were fewer incidents of bullying when the children were closely watched by the lunchtime supervisors. In the final interview, the second teacher stated that behaviour in the class had deteriorated and that 'there's a real containing exercise this year'. It seems a shame that the peer mediation programme was not implemented in ways that might have had an impact on student levels of bullying and disruption. By the end of the programme, this head was at least aware of where things had gone wrong, and was keen to put things right: 'I think in hindsight, I think I would perhaps have given more training to the members of staff before we started moving into it. I think . . . that mediation, the skill of mediation training with a group of children is far higher than I think perhaps we had recognized.'

This, at least, is a stronger point at which to end the programme than in School Three, where there was no recognition of any problem and certainly no desire to find a solution.

Similar themes emerge from other commentaries and research into peer mediation. Sellman (2002) in an article on peer mediation, school culture and sustainability notes that, 'there is a link between school culture, including how members of staff regulate conflict and the chances of peer mediation projects being successful' (Sellman, 2002: 7). Referring to the work of Bernstein (1977) he suggests that schools can be placed on a spectrum with strong classification and framing at one end, and weak classification and framing at the other end. Those who demonstrate strong classification and framing locate authority and control with the teacher. In these schools it is the teachers' responsibility to evaluate conflicts and arbitrate an appropriate resolution, which may include punishment for one or more parties. There is little scope for student voice, with conflict viewed as something to be avoided through rules and sanctions. Those who demonstrate weak classification and framing provide students with training and opportunities to resolve conflicts for themselves. In these schools there is a belief that meaningful and lasting resolution of conflicts rests on all parties being involved in a problem-solving approach to conflict. As Sellman (2002: 9) points out, 'such an approach allows greater scope for pupil voice'. He goes on: 'Peer mediation will encounter great difficulty in having any effect in a school with strong classification and framing; at best it will be a discrete "bolt-on" feature' (Sellman, 2002: 9).

He cites research analysing peer mediation schemes in Scotland which shows that a frequent obstacle to the implementation and sustenance of peer mediation included teachers' unwillingness to modify their own views of authority and to model the relevant skills themselves:

> In such a culture there is a clash of approaches to the regulation of conflict. There is a clash because peer mediation becomes a discrete entity, usually oriented towards playground disputes, with little relevance to other areas of school. This organisation causes problems for pupils, who may struggle to differentiate between times and spaces suitable for arbitration and those suitable for peer mediation.
> (Sellman, 2002: 9)

Finally, he turns his attention to the sustainability of peer mediation programmes in school, and asserts that, 'Peer mediation as part of a long-term systemic analysis of school development is more sustainable' (Sellman, 2002: 10). Once again, links are made between peer mediation, school ethos, and a well-conceived and executed plan of school development.

Kathy Bickmore, a Canadian expert in citizenship and conflict resolution in schools, writes similarly about the need for a particular set of values and practices to underpin peer mediation. Reviewing the ways in which peer mediation was implemented in six Canadian elementary schools in the same urban school district (Bickmore, 2001) she identifies a conceptual framework for studying citizenship education in schools, based in part on recent literature on service learning. In this conceptual framework, democratic citizenship has three central components: modelling, critical reasoning, and sharing authority with students. The peer mediation programme that was implemented in the six schools was designed to foster leadership amongst diverse young people, and to develop student's capacities as responsible citizens through being given tangible responsibility, specifically the power to carry out peer-conflict management activities. In practice, as the programmes developed, some schools did not share responsibility with any of their student mediators, and others shared power only with the kinds of children already seen as 'good students'. Only two of the six schools contained elements of authority-sharing by the end of the implementation period.

Two of the schools, Atlantic and Browncroft Schools, emphasized peacemaking as part of community building, without involving the student mediators in much critical thinking, problem solving, or autonomous action. In Atlantic School, the mediators were disproportionately white/Anglo and female. They had little opportunity to think critically together or take autonomous initiative, and Bickmore points out that, 'their peacekeeping seemed considerably less than democratic: mediators often helped adults to *limit* the autonomy of their peers' (Bickmore, 2001: 147). In Browncroft School, student behaviour was managed primarily by teachers and principals, and trained peer mediators did not have many opportunities for providing a service. The conflict resolution training in this school emphasized 'student skill development and norms of polite behaviour, rather than student-centred peer mediation' (Bickmore, 2001: 147). When asked what mediation involved, the students at Browncroft School told a researcher, 'we tell students not to fight'. While role-playing mediation they failed to go through a series of problem-solving steps, substituting instead peer pressure to apologize and shake hands. The peer mediation coordinator in this school had assertive discipline expectations and consequences on her classroom wall. Bickmore notes that, 'Assertive discipline's emphasis on inflexible rules and teacher control seems quite contradictory to the spirit and practice of peer mediation, but no student, teacher, or administrator remarked on any such tensions during observations or interviews: all assumed that this program's emphasis should be on changing *children's* behaviour, not on changing adults' behavior or authority relations' (Bickmore, 2001: 147). Citizenship education in these two schools emphasized 'student compliance, the dominant culture's middle-class manners, and student's acquisition of narrow skills more than the development of democratic initiative or organisational change' (Bickmore, 2001: 148).

Bickmore points out that Clover School was typical of North American schools with peer mediation schemes, in that several adults in school were reluctant to allow mediators time or support to offer their services (either in their own classrooms or beyond), except during lunch and break times. Although the teachers in Dixon Schools were 'surprised and delighted' with how effective the newly trained mediators were at assisting peers to resolve conflicts, the students who were chosen to be mediators were 'academically successful students who rarely got into trouble' (Bickmore, 2001: 152). Bickmore cites Kahne and Westheimer (1996: 599) who critique simplistic notions of empowerment that underlie some service programs, and notes that:

> Increasing student's self esteem through serving 'those less fortunate', without helping them to understand and reflect critically on the reasons for these people's troubles – as possibly reinforcing relatively privileged students' unearned sense of superiority and bypassing important learning opportunities.

She reflects on the links between culture and behaviour in schools, asking herself, 'To what degree might peer mediation serve as an unintended disseminator of culturally loaded and problematised "good behaviour models?"' (Bickmore, 2001: 149). Any citizenship education program coexists with the hidden curriculum, and it is therefore essential that students who are chosen to be mediators reflect the diversity of the student body. In the six schools under review here, the mediators were representative in two cases. Students who became mediators in Ellison and Fairview school came from all sectors of the school's community, and ranged from those whose goals and behaviours were in alignment with dominant school values, to those whose goals and behaviours were set in opposition to the school. Diverse students in these programmes drew upon 'different personal histories and strengths' and on their experiences as members of very different social and ethnic communities within and outside of school. In Ellison School, the conflict resolution advisor (peer mediation coordinator) served on the school's discipline committee, and had the agreement of most staff and parents to incorporate mediation into the school's discipline process. In this school, mediators and teachers reported that virtually 100 per cent of conflicts in which mediators assisted were resolved completely, so that those problems did not resurface.

Despite these more promising findings in two of the six schools, Bickmore nevertheless ends the paper by noting that by the end of the implementation period none of the schools had been able to support the mediators to develop autonomy by sharing authority and making joint decisions in a sustained way. She ends with a salutary reminder:

> There is a heavy weight of tradition and habit in schools, exacerbated by the newly strengthened demands for centrally controlled academic testing, that can get in the way of democratisation efforts. By being explicit about the cultural and political goals underlying peer mediation programmes, educators may be more able to focus their energies on the important challenges, thereby helping to displace this weight to some degree and making a little more space for learning democracy.
>
> (Bickmore, 2001: 160)

Conclusion

This chapter has reviewed attitudes towards power, control, conflict and childhood in order to illuminate the concept of student voice in the context of citizenship and peer mediation. It has focused on attitudes in schools, as well as in wider society, in order to reflect on some of the issues behind the successful implementation of peer mediation. It has used case studies of circle time and peer mediation in schools to illustrate some of the complex ways in which attitudes and values play out in the everyday lives of children and adults in schools. Although there is much to generate concern amongst those who wish to engage with student voice in schools, it is also encouraging that rare schools do exist which appear able, despite all the odds, to create a relatively safe and empowering space for young people to experience authentic education for citizenship, enabling them to practise effective conflict resolution, autonomous decision making, and a certain degree of power sharing.

6   A case study of peer mediation in Stanville Primary School

Introduction

The first case study of peer mediation to be presented here is of Stanville Primary School in Birmingham, UK. This chapter and the following chapter will present case studies of peer mediation in a school and in a project involving a number of schools. The case studies were chosen as they were all known to have sustained involvement in peer mediation over a number of years. Analysis of data from each case centres around the following research questions:

- How did this school/project go about establishing peer mediation?
- How has peer mediation in this context evolved over the years?
- What were the reasons for developing peer mediation in the first place?
- Has peer mediation been successful in achieving the aims of those who set it up?
- Have there been any unexpected benefits?
- What have been the drawbacks or difficulties in implementing peer mediation in this context?
- How were any challenges responded to?

These research questions will be addressed in a variety of ways through each case study, with interviews and documentary analysis used as key methods for data collection. Stanville School is within five miles of the centre of Birmingham, UK, and provides education for children between the ages of three and 11. One quarter of its intake is British minority ethnic and the number of children who take free school meals is above the national average. Birmingham is the second city in the UK, after London. It has a population of around five million, and has a strong industrial heritage, which is now in decline. It has recently undergone substantial regeneration and has much improved leisure and business facilities.

The author has been involved with this school for around seven years, and has been instrumental in providing peer mediation trainers and teaching materials for the annual training of students that takes place in the summer term. She provided training for the first group of mediators herself in 1999. In November 2001, this school was the host school of the Birmingham-wide conference for peer mediators, whose findings are reported in Chapter Two.

This chapter is based on a visit to the school in July 2006. Documentation about peer mediation was collected at this time, and a number of interviews were carried out. Interviewees included Lynne Whiteoak, a member of the senior leadership team, and special educational needs/inclusion coordinator (SENCO), Helen Watton, assistant SENCO and peer mediation coordinator, three parents of children who had been mediators in the school, and six mediators, two from each of years four (eight-to-nine-year-olds) to six (10-to-11-year-olds). Helen Watton is a senior member of the team of teaching assistants in the school and is a school mentor. She has a particular interest in social and emotional behavioural difficulties, and her insights into the lives of children and families in the school's community have undoubtedly added value to the peer-mediation project in this school over the years.

The peer-mediation project began in this school in 1999. It was initially identified as a response to the needs of key stage two (seven to 11) children at lunchtimes. Lunchtimes were providing a particular challenge for certain children as they contained 40 minutes of unstructured playtime. The lunchtime supervisors (non-teaching support staff) were also experiencing difficulties, with no play equipment and children involved in high levels of conflict. The lunchtime supervisors did not know how to respond to children's 'tales' and found it even more difficult to 'get to the truth'. Children's arguments were spilling into the afternoons, with teachers sometimes taking up to 20 minutes to sort out problems. None of this was setting the right tone for the afternoon's lessons. Lynne Whiteoak notes that, in addition, 'society has changed, people are looking out for themselves. Children are influenced by the media, TV, lots of arguments, shouting.' Peer mediation was seen as a way of overcoming some of these difficulties.

The school began by training 25 key stage two children, aged between nine and 10, to offer a service to all other children in the school at lunchtimes. Lunchtime supervisors were also trained in strategies for effective conflict resolution, and in ways of supporting an emerging peer mediation service. It was not long before lunchtime supervisors were offering mediation to children, 'or do you want us to decide who is right and wrong?' At first, the mediators were overwhelmed, with long queues, but then it became quieter.

Developing and sustaining peer mediation

At the time of the visit there were 50 trained mediators in key stage two, with training for key stage one mediators (seven-year-olds) planned for the following September. The promises and rules that the Stanville mediators use when mediating are shown in Box 6.1. The four-step process that they follow is shown in Box 6.2. Essentially they use this model to facilitate dispute resolution amongst peers, without making judgements or directing the outcomes of the dispute. The mediators have a small book made out of card with notes on each of four pages as an *aide mémoire*.

Box 6.1   *Stanville mediators' promises and rules*

Promises and Rules

Our promises
We will be fair – we won't take sides.
We won't tell you what to do.
We will keep it private unless it is harmful to you or others.

Your rules
Allow each other to speak without butting in.
No name calling or swearing.
Talk about the problem from your own point of view – try not to blame or accuse other people.

The lunchtime supervisors issue children with tokens for them to be allowed to go in and access mediation during outdoor play at lunchtime. Sometimes teachers refer children to mediation during the lunch hour. Children can also access the service by going to stand at special friendship bus stops, which are placed in known areas of the playground, and are 'staffed' by mediators who also function as play leaders and friendship helpers. Children recognize mediators because they wear a special jumper, an ID badge and a mediator's cap. Mediators either mediate *in situ* on the playground, or else they direct disputants to a room in school that has been especially set aside at lunchtimes for mediation. The mediation room is staffed by pairs of mediators who provide a service on a rota basis. When it is quiet, they play games that the SENCO has provided for them to use whilst they are waiting. When mediations are completed, a brief outline of the nature of the dispute and its outcome are recorded in a folder, along with the names of the disputants. The disputants sign the agreement, as do the mediators. There are regular 10-minute meetings with Lynne, Helen, and/or, Mrs Lowe, the senior lunchtime supervisor, to discuss the progress that the mediators are making, and to iron out any difficulties that might emerge.

After the first year, peer mediation training switched to key stage one (seven-year-olds) as it was felt that these younger children would gain valuable social and emotional skills from the process. Training was provided over five afternoons, with the children being offered certificates to celebrate their achievements. This proved to be highly successful and training continued to

---

Box 6.2 *Stanville mediation process*

Welcome and introduction
Welcome them to mediation
Tell them your names
Ask for their names

Mediator's promises
We won't gossip
We won't take sides
We won't tell you what to do

Disputants' rules
Speak one at a time and don't interrupt each other
Speak with respect
Don't blame each other

CHECK THEY AGREE

Finding out the facts
Find out who wants to go first
Ask them for their side of the story
Feedback
Ask the other person for their side of the story
Feedback

Finding out about their feelings
Ask person A how they feel
Ask person B if they can see how person A feels
Repeat for person B

Problem solving
Ask for solutions
Ask them to agree on a solution

END MEDIATION

---

be provided for key stage one children on an annual basis, with top-up training for mediators as they entered key stage two. Mediators were then able to offer a service within their own key stage, although it is not unheard of for older children to ask younger mediators for help. The training is supported with worksheets for very young children, with cloze exercises and pictures to colour to get them used to the language and concepts of mediation.

Lynne Whiteoak, reflected on the reasons behind the ongoing success of peer mediation in the school during her interview. She felt that it is important to continue to keep the profile of peer mediation high, with regular assemblies to remind children in the school what the service can offer, and noticeboards and displays throughout the school giving information about peer mediation and celebrating its success. Figure 6.1 shows a picture of a noticeboard, taken during the visit to the school. This profile of peer mediation in the school was particularly enhanced through the Birmingham-wide conference in 2001 discussed in Chapter Two. The day was enjoyable for the mediators as they were able to meet other young mediators from across the city, and they appreciated being treated as young adults. The children appreciated the fact that the conference was held in a hotel and that they were made aware of the ways in which their developing skills could be used within their communities and future workplaces.

Figure 6.1 Picture of a noticeboard in Stanville School

Lynne felt that peer mediation cannot be successful unless circle time is firmly in place in every classroom in the school (see Chapter 5). Peer mediation also needs to be run alongside other initiatives to support vulnerable children. In Stanville, for example, they have a Lunchtime Buddy Room, where children can eat lunch at a table with adults and learn to play in a small protected environment before going out into the playground. Lunchtime colouring and craft clubs have also been started by lunchtime supervisors and

parents as a way of involving children who otherwise might experience difficulties with unstructured play. Some children have been given jobs to do at
lunchtime to enhance their feelings of self-confidence and responsibility
within their school community. Children with difficulties with literacy and
numeracy have been supported with an alternative curriculum for some of
the time in the afternoons. Rather than being given yet more literacy and
numeracy support (as would be the case in many schools) the school
approached a local recruitment agency, Pertemps, to come into school and
provide coaching and team building for the children. The children were able
to go on to work with parents in school on craft activities, and sold their crafts
and hanging baskets in the community as part of a community enterprise
initiative, thus linking back into literacy and numeracy skills.

The strong partnership with parents is in evidence in most of the
initiatives that the school takes on. It clearly places a high priority on this
work. The parents of peer mediators Amy Robinson, Michael Ravenscroft and
Bethany Pereira provided an interview as part of this case study. All of them
worked or volunteered in the school in one capacity or another, and had
strong relationships with the school. Lynne Whiteoak is aware of the need for
support and training amongst many of the school's young parents, and has
made links with Solihull Further Education College (a post-16 provider) in
order to provide accredited courses on the school premises during the school
day in subjects like first aid, beauty care and becoming a teaching assistant.
The school also runs family learning sessions, with a parent and a child
working together on a task. All of these approaches combine with peer
mediation to create an environment in which mutual care and active citizenship can thrive. Lynne feels that this is in part due to the awareness raising
that took place during the in-service training that was provided for all
teaching and support staff (many of whom are parents) in the initial stages of
establishing peer mediation in the school. Peer mediation, according to
Lynne, initiated 'a layered approach', which has 'enhanced the curriculum for
vulnerable children'. She feels that for peer mediation to be successful, the
ethos of the school must be right. Peer mediation 'offers firm foundations' but
it can't stand alone. Its philosophy has to permeate other initiatives.

The school's strengths were noted by Ofsted in 2005 as providing, 'outstanding care, guidance and support' to all pupils who attend. They highlighted the role of peer mediators in particular: 'Children's contribution to
the community is outstanding. Many pupils undertake demanding roles in
the school, for example, as highly effective peer mediators.'

Peer mediation has featured annually on the school's improvement plan,
and has therefore benefited from prioritized funding and staff time. It has also
been the subject of regular staff meetings. Staff meet annually to agree their
collective aims, in line with the school's vision statement. The collective aims
for 2006/7 are shown in Table 6.1, and demonstrate once more the ways in

which this school creates an environment in which peer mediation can thrive.

The school has also provided a hub for networking around issues of inclusion with three primary schools, a special school and a secondary school in their locality. Through the Stanville Inclusion Network, peer tutoring, family learning, drama and dance projects have been developed through a consortium-based approach. The school has been able to reach out to other schools in its community to share successes and build on strengths.

Table 6.1 The staff's aims 2006/7

Environment	To provide a safe, stimulating and well-resources learning environment which is friendly and encourages pupils to make the most of their abilities and potential
Academic ability and self-esteem	To encourage independence, confidence, creativity and a love of learning which enables pupils to develop their own self-esteem and achieve their full academic potential.
	To provide opportunities for pupils to learn and develop their social skills, to include:
	• Consideration, respect and tolerance of each other • Pride in their school and each other • Understanding of the importance of teamwork and co-operation • Valuing themselves as a member of society
Family and community	To build on strong links with families and the wider community, and to support pupils to develop an appreciation of their role and responsibilities within their family and wider community.

Meet the mediators

Year six mediators

The year six mediators were trained when they were in year two, and have been mediating ever since. They remember that their training involved using cards as prompts during activities, and that they did lots of role plays and memorizing the rules. They do less mediation now because the younger mediators are in post – they probably do around one every three months. They are aware of the limits of their role; teachers mediate conflict during morning break and the deputy head is responsible for dealing with serious incidents.

Stephanie Christie loves dogs and hates squash. Good things about mediation are that you can find out how to help people and it is great when people make friends. Bad things are when you feel that you are being bossy (enforcing the rules of mediation) and when people don't listen to you.

James Rice loves football and doesn't know what he hates. Good things about mediation are that you don't have to do it very often (?!) and that most of the time they make friends. Bad things are that it can be boring, and people make it hard by making things up (wasting your time) and by walking out. James has dealt with a fight before but only when they had calmed down. It was hard to get them to sit next to each other at first. He feels that there is less of a need for mediation in school nowadays as most children know how to do it for themselves without the aid of a mediator.

Amy Robinson loves horses and hates sprouts. She likes helping people to make friends, but is pleased that she does not have to mediate very often any more. She doesn't like having to try not to get involved (remain impartial). Like Stephanie, she doesn't like feeling bossy, and doesn't like it when people don't listen. Amy's mum, Carol, notes that Amy has always been confident and that she enjoyed being a mediator, taking her responsibilities very seriously. Her younger sister, Emily, was also trained as a mediator. Helping to sort out playground squabbles has made Emily more assertive, and has encouraged her to talk to adults and children she doesn't know. Amy and Emily's mum notes that, 'Both my children wear their mediator cap and jumper with pride.'

Year five mediators

The year five mediators were trained in year two. They remember spending time learning the rules of mediation during their training, and doing a role play in the actual playground. Through the daily rota, they are each on duty in the mediation room once a month. While on duty they look out of the window to see if anyone is having a dispute, or they sometimes go outside. Fights are separated by lunchtime supervisors but mediators can step in to help those involved to resolve their difficulties when they have calmed down a bit. People argue about games and people getting pushed. People get called names, sometimes racist names, but mediators challenge name calling around the school and teachers always become involved when there is a racist incident. One child in school who has ADHD uses mediation almost every day. Mediators in his class also help the teacher when he has problems in lessons.

Bethany Pereira loves Bratz dolls, and hates slugs. She likes being a mediator, and being allowed to come in at lunchtime when it is really hot or cold. You get to feel grown up and mature sorting people's arguments out. She doesn't like it when disputants call you names, even though you are trying to help them, or when they say that you are lying. She doesn't like it either when they refuse to come in, or waste all of your playtime. Her mum, Annette Pereira, is clear about the benefits of peer mediation for her daughter:

As the parent of a trained mediator I have been very impressed with the positive and effective training skills my daughter has undertaken. Being a mediator has helped my daughter to grow in confidence, develop self-help skills, become aware of the importance of giving everyone a fair hearing, and develop listening skills. In addition the promises mediators make, and the rules of being mediated, enable the children to develop positive strategies to help others resolve disputes. Moreover, they encourage children to be fair, to not be judgemental and to be able to work as part of a team, all of which are essential life skills which will enable them to grow as they mature. My daughter enjoys being a mediator and her self-esteem grows and develops each time she is able to help other children to become friends again.

Hollie Jeynes Langford loves football and hates wasps. Being a mediator makes her feel more grown up and mature, but she doesn't like it when disputants are hurtful, or 'say that we are bossing them around'. She doesn't like long mediation meetings, or dealing with disputants who refuse to come in or say that she is lying. She feels that, 'some teachers don't listen to you' so that, 'mediators have to sort it out.'

Luke Jeynes Langford loves football and YU-GI-OH (a card game). He hates doing his room. He likes it when no one comes to mediation (!). He likes being able to draw and 'be nice'. He doesn't like getting hurt or told off as a mediator.

Lee Hill loves football, and the game Truth or Dare? He hates fish and some chocolate, like Turkish Delight. He likes mediation when he gets merits and good mediation results. He feels that 'when we have to mediate, it makes us more mature', although he also likes it when he is not on duty, as he loves his playtime.

Year four mediators

Out of the year four mediators, only Curtis Choudhury was available for interview. He loves cheese and hates being told off. During mediations he likes making people happy and helping people to be friends. He finds it fun. He doesn't like it when 'people say that you are on a side'. Curtis mediated every day recently to support two boys with a particular problem. He talked to the teacher about it and the problem was sorted. He doesn't feel that people treat mediators differently, as there are 'lots of mediators in school'. He does feel that children in school like mediators because 'we sort problems out and we are not horrible to people'. He describes a much broader scope for mediation than the others, possibly reflecting his ability level and enhanced support from his class teacher, 'We also help people with other problems, like not doing work or not eating dinner or when someone's Nan has died.'

Mediators now at secondary school

Although it was not possible to meet a mediator who had moved on to secondary school, the school provided a written statement from a former student. Michael Ravenscroft (now in year seven of a local secondary school) felt that peer mediation had helped in the transition to his next phase of schooling: 'I felt proud when I became a mediator. Being a mediator was fun and taught me how to sort problems out. This helped me move to secondary school by giving me essential communication skills.'

His mum, Mrs R Ravenscroft, was equally positive about the ways in which peer mediation had helped her son:

> When my son was chosen to be a mediator, I felt very proud of him. Being a shy child, I felt that it helped him to become more confident to approach his peers, and to help them with their disputes if they had any. He would tell me when he was on duty and be pleased to wear his jumper and cap. I believe that the experience was rewarding for Michael and hope that many more children will have the same experience as he had at Stanville School with regards to being a mediator.

Outcomes of peer mediation

Lynne Whiteoak feels that peer mediation has been part of an evolving ethos in her school. It is clear that peer mediation has been a central part of achieving the outcomes of the UK government's Every Child Matters (ECM) agenda. It helps the children to stay safe through the reduction of conflict; it enables mediators (and cooperative disputants) to make a positive contribution to a peaceful school community; it helps children to acquire conflict-resolution skills that are applicable in the home and workplace and it contributes to children's feelings of wellbeing, happiness self-esteem and inclusion. It has also contributed to an emerging culture of active citizenship in the school, with a new project to train children as park rangers in the local community under development, for example.

The peer mediators have carried mediation skills forward into their classrooms and homes. During her interview Lynne gave an example of a mediator who went on a visit to his new secondary school as part of the induction process. Whilst being shown around the school, he offered to mediate for two boys who were two years older than him, with a successful outcome!. The head of the year seven (first year secondary) phoned the primary school and the mediator's parents to congratulate them. Lynne notes that the children are using their peer mediation skills at home with siblings and parents. She summarizes by saying that the school is 'considerably calmer' now. This is echoed by Helen Watton who says that the students in the school are very mature and self-confident. Peer mediation has been 'empowering for them'. In the eight years during which peer mediation has been operational there has been an 'unbelievable difference to the school'.

The parents feel that the mediators' training has stayed with them. One of them suggested that it is like a mirror that the student can hold up in times of stress. Running the peer mediation scheme has given the students a sense of responsibility – having to keep to the rota, even when play outside seems more attractive. Their children all know what they want to do in future careers – and the parents reflect that mediating may have helped them to feel more able to take control of their future. They have noticed that their children tend to deal better with problems. When they mediate at home, they sometimes challenge their parents, saying, 'it is my turn to speak'. As one of the parents points out: 'It makes you think, you've got to listen to them.'

These parents were not concerned about child safety. They are aware that there are always adults in the next room who can intervene if necessary. They are also not concerned about children having time off their normal curriculum for training, 'Children need to learn other things, I am pleased to have had the opportunity.'

Anne Lowe, the senior lunchtime supervisor, worked in the school both before and after mediation was put in place. She feels that the school is now 'much calmer'. The visit took place in the final week of term, and, as she pointed out, unlike many schools at that time of year, there was still a calm atmosphere. She reflected that 'Most children can sort themselves out. Children are better at sorting out other children's problems. They can avoid punishment, and can deal with petty things that adults don't think are important.'

Conclusion

Stanville is clearly a success story for peer mediation. These success stories are rarer than one would hope, and it is to the school's credit that it has persevered with its original vision of peaceful lunchtimes as well as continuing to innovate and evolve. The outcomes for the school after seven years go way beyond the resolution of peer disputes at lunchtimes – children have acquired and internalized key social and affective skills, with vulnerable children having gained the most. It is interesting to note the mediators' occasional ambivalence towards the mediation process, with many of them missing their playtimes and feeling the negative as well as the positive side of carrying certain responsibilities on behalf of their peers. These issues will no doubt be dealt with as part of the school's ongoing review of peer mediation. Perhaps they will structure weekly meetings to include team games and fun activities, or maybe they will give the mediators certain treats and rewards (ice-skating, cinema, parties ...). They may also decide to ensure that the role of the mediator doesn't extend beyond a year's service. What they have been able to demonstrate, however, is a reflective and engaged approach to improving the social and educational outcomes of the children in their school, which will carry them through any difficulties.

7 A case study of peer mediation in Handsworth Association of Schools

Introduction

The second case study of peer mediation to be presented here is of Handsworth Association of Schools (HAS). This association is made up of six secondary schools (for students aged between 11 and 16 or 18) and 24 primary schools (for children aged between three and 11). It is part of Birmingham local authority's community education provision, and serves an area high in social deprivation and ethnic diversity. Handsworth Association of Schools is based in a community building in the grounds of one of the primary schools, and employs a small number of staff to manage various projects on behalf of the partnership schools. These include parent partnership, peer mediation, mentoring and a Young People's Parliament.

The research questions for this case study are as before, namely:

- How did this school/project go about establishing peer mediation?
- How has peer mediation in this context evolved over the years?
- What were the reasons for developing peer mediation in the first place?
- Has peer mediation been successful in achieving the aims of those who set it up?
- Have there been any unexpected benefits?
- What have been the drawbacks or difficulties in implementing peer mediation in this context?
- How were any challenges responded to?

This case study is based on interviews carried out in July 2006 and notes taken by the Catalyst peer mediation trainers who were central in setting up and supporting this project, Rosie Norwood and Cath Barker. Interviewees included Anita Harding, the HAS coordinator, Moira Foster Brown, headteacher of Birchfield Junior and Infants Community School, and Chair of the HAS, and Ken Brown, learning mentor and peer mediation coordinator from Welford Junior and Infant School.

Developing and sustaining peer mediation

This section is based primarily on the interview with Anita Harding, the HAS coordinator. The first mediators were trained by Catalyst Conflict and Change Ltd (www.catalystconflictandchange.org) in 2000. Single Regeneration Budget (SRB) community safety monies were used. Initially the budget was small, involving 10 schools. There were two days of training for peer mediation coordinators (teachers) from the 10 schools to begin with, followed by two days of training for lunchtime supervisors in the 10 schools, and then five lots of three-day training courses for children in year five (nine-to-10-year-olds). Each school paired up with another school for the training of children to reduce costs, and to encourage partnership and links across the 10 schools. Published materials were used by Catalyst's trainers as a basis of the work with children (Stacey, 2001) and covered team-building activities, listening activities, circle games, peer mediation role play, and designing the peer mediation service. Students were taught about the situations where peer mediation would and would not be appropriate. Training for teachers looked at mediation as a process of dispute resolution in schools, and at school culture and ethos. It used role play to encourage teachers to engage with the complexities of non-adversarial dispute resolution. Training with lunchtime supervisors focused similarly on mediation role play, but also looked at the particular challenges of managing student behaviour and conflicts during break and lunchtimes. All of the training was provided off-site in order to raise the status of the activities that were being promoted.

Anita admits that peer mediation was initially introduced for pragmatic reasons, to 'address lunchtime issues', and enable in quieter playgrounds. The issues to be resolved included shouting by lunchtime supervisors, insufficient time to listen to young people, and teachers being overburdened in the afternoons by children who had been in disputes over lunchtime. In her interview, Anita recalled that, 'in my final year as a primary teacher I had a particular young lady who always had issues on a Friday lunchtime. Friday afternoons were always taken up with resolving her disputes – badly, because adult intervention didn't seem to help.' As the project has gone on, however, Anita points out that, 'priorities have changed' with the HAS more concerned with supporting young people to become more involved in resolving their own issues, and learning to take more responsibility.

Around half of the schools from the initial 10-school project maintained the service the following year retraining the next lot of mediators themselves. Those schools that continued under their own steam were very strongly committed, with peer mediation as a visible presence in schools, but the others needed more than a one-off input. A major problem with the first phase of the project, according to Anita Harding, was that it was teacher-led, with busy teachers not always able to maintain the essential weekly meetings with students.

A decision was made in 2002 to extend the project to all schools in Handsworth and Ladywood, which was the area covered by the new round of SRB funding (SRB6). The decision was based on the success of the first ten-school project. As part of gaining this funding the peer mediators went to ward meetings to make a case to local councillors and residents. This was certainly an eye opener for the mediators, who were shocked at the way that some of the adults in those meetings conducted themselves. Several of them commented later that the adults needed to be taught how to maintain ground rules for public discussion, and the teachers involved used this as an opportunity to engage them in reflection on the implications of free speech and local democracy! Following this, a new code of practice on appropriate behaviour in meetings was drawn up and implemented. As Anita points out, 'Young people with these skills have an important role to play in the future of this community.'

The decision to extend the project coincided with the introduction of learning mentors into schools in Birmingham. Learning mentors are provided with extensive training, and in Handsworth this was supplemented with training in conflict resolution skills, and in coordinating a peer mediation service. Thirty learning mentors based in Handsworth schools, many of whom were young men, agreed to coordinate peer mediation in their schools. A schedule for training peer mediators was drawn up as before, with schools pairing up to receive three days of training for year five (nine-to-10-year-old) students. At this stage, the training for students was facilitated by the Catalyst trainers, although it was anticipated that the mentors (who were observing this work with students) would provide the training the following year. In many ways, peer mediation provided an ideal first project for the mentors, as it used a highly structured approach, building on the best practice and resources that the teachers had developed in the previous year.

Catalyst Conflict and Change then worked with the Handsworth Association of Schools in the following year to design a staged exit strategy that would enable the learning mentors to take this work forward unaided. The learning mentors worked together in the same pairs as before to offer the training to the new year-five peer mediators. The original Catalyst trainers delivered half of the training at the request of the learning mentors. A tailor-made handbook was produced by and for the Handsworth schools in association with Catalyst. Most of the mentors enjoyed providing half of the training themselves and being able to 'run with' the project in their schools. A few of them, however, felt burdened with the role, as stated by Cath Barker, a trainer from Catalyst, in her notes:

Initially the primary mediation schemes had a teacher co-ordinator supported by a learning mentor. Over the years the learning mentors have largely taken on this role themselves. Many fully embraced this role, but some felt burdened by doing it alone. They were encouraged to invite another member of staff to share the role and additional training was put on for these staff.

In the following year the learning mentors successfully carried out the training for the new year five students themselves. This work was supported by the Handsworth Group of Schools through a peer mediation conference that was held at the Council House in Birmingham city centre. The conference was attended by the leader of the council and the Lord Mayor. The aim of the conference was to celebrate the achievements of the young people and the learning mentors, and to raise the profile of their work.

Anita believes that the learning mentors are now really strong. They are continuing to coordinate peer mediation in their schools, with the HAS providing practical resources such as mediator badges and caps. Each school has been given a mediator bench to put in the playground. Cath Barker notes that the schools that give mediation the highest profile tend to be the most successful. She recognizes that Handsworth schools have been given an unprecedented amount of support to get peer mediation up and running. This has taken the form of funding, (friendly) pressure and regular visits from Anita and the HAS project workers. If a school goes quiet, a visit is arranged to keep the momentum going. The HAS provides annual training for new staff, learning mentors and lunchtime supervisors and there is a twice-yearly networking meeting for all Handsworth schools involved in this project. Some schools 'have been lost' (three out of the 24 primary schools) but it has become normal for schools to come in and go out of the project according to staffing and other school-related issues. Anita Harding feels that the learning mentors are now able to run the project themselves, and that it has greatly contributed to their confidence, 'The learning mentors are now taking peer mediation in new directions in their schools, expanding the numbers of student trained, and so on. The headteachers have fed back that they do have quieter playgrounds.'

Work with the secondary schools has been more problematic and that is where Anita feels development is needed. One of the schools has started to support peer mediation informally, but without an official mediation service. In another school the result was even more disappointing, with a cohort of peer mediators trained by Catalyst and ready to go but with no member of staff able to commit to their ongoing support. The young people's enthusiasm was soon thwarted. Attempts are currently being made to resurrect these young people's skills through a peer mentoring service. Anita Harding feels that for peer mediation to be successful, 'there has to be a designated member of staff. In our enthusiasm to get it into every school some children were let down.' Cath Barker worked with two of the secondary schools, and notes that there were a variety of reasons why peer mediation did not really take off. These include a lack of designated space in school, decisions at senior management level being delayed beyond a point which was acceptable to the mediators, and learning mentors feeling isolated with their role.

Outcomes of peer mediation

Peer Mediation at Birchfield Junior and Infants Community School

Moira Foster Brown, the headteacher of one of the 24 HAS schools, feels that, 'peer mediation has made a difference to children's self-esteem and the way that teachers and students view playtime'. It has also brought out some important issues. For example, teachers have become increasingly aware that children are very good at maintaining friendships within their own groups of friends, but they are not always as welcoming to new students, including asylum seekers. Peer mediation has provided a context for these issues to be explored and the school has been able to respond through learning and teaching strategies.

Academic achievement has improved dramatically in this school over the past few years (according to SAT scores). Moira feels that this is due to children's increased feelings of confidence and empowerment and a more peaceful environment in school. Peer mediators tend to put themselves forward for other roles in the school, and they are allowed to run the school for a day in July. This has become part of school culture, with all students knowing that this is one of the privileges that peer mediators can look forward to. Mediators have trained other children and they are involved in regular assemblies on a theme of conflict resolution. The school would like to do more to develop this work with younger children.

Moira notes that it is important to keep improving links with parents and with teaching in other areas of the curriculum. The school has just completed a project exploring feelings about conflict, for example, from the local to the global. Challenges include the need to provide training for new members of staff, and top-up training for all staff. Now that the learning mentors are coordinating peer mediation in the school, there is a danger that teaching staff could be one stage removed from live issues and conflicts that children in the school are faced with. This makes it imperative for the school to maintain good systems for communication and translating shared values into lived experience.

Peer Mediation at Welford Junior and Infants School

Ken Brown, the learning mentor and peer mediation coordinator, feels that the playground is now a calmer place. Problems don't escalate in the way they used to and teachers have noted some positive changes in peer mediators, including raised self-esteem and confidence. He acknowledges that a lot of the mediators didn't get on with each other at the beginning but that they are now willing to work as a team. Some of them had problems with their own temper but they have learnt to control it, knowing that they would be in the spotlight.

Mediation is popular with disputants in the playground as it is a better option than being sent to the headteacher. Despite this, the service was less used at the time of the interview than previously, as children learnt to use the skills for themselves. They 'don't need the help of the mediators as often now'.

Both teachers and children give peer mediation a high profile in this school, and this is at the root of its success, according to Ken. The peer mediators are given rewards to thank them for their time and hard work (the previous term they had been bowling) and there are more children who want to be mediators than are needed. Ken has agreed that he will provide additional training for these children. He is also devising a package of training for lunchtime supervisors with the senior lunchtime supervisor. The training will demonstrate how peer mediation can make their jobs easier, leaving them free to deal with more serious issues and promote positive play.

Conclusion

This case study is different from the previous one in that it involves an association of schools with an existing infrastructure and set of procedures for collaborative working. The schools have the benefit of full-time workers to access and administer external funding and to ensure that project outcomes are met. The schools have not had to raise funds or use their own resources in order to develop peer mediation. There have also been certain economies of scale, with joint conferences and shared student/teacher/learning mentor/ lunchtime supervisor training. The effects of this are 20 thriving peer mediation projects in one of the most socially deprived urban communities in the UK. Outcomes have included more peaceful playgrounds, enhanced skills and attainment, raised self-esteem, greater impulse control and an empowered group of learning mentors. Challenges to be addressed include the need to ensure that peer mediation does not become isolated from teaching staff and issues of teaching and learning, and the need to ensure that learning mentors are fully supported in their role as school peer mediation coordinators. This needs to be a whole-staff responsibility, and is in evidence in the schools which demonstrate best practice. A further consideration is the need for schools to evolve their own systems of working. These schools have been given a strong start, and it is appropriate that support is now at a lower level so that they can find their own motivations and ways of working that best suit their needs and localized school context.

8   Researching peer mediation

Introduction

This penultimate chapter provides an overview of research into peer mediation, some of which has appeared in earlier chapters, although duplication will be avoided where possible. It will then go on to suggest that much of the methodology that has been used to evaluate peer mediation in the past contains flaws, and that these will need to be addressed if research into peer mediation is to make a significant contribution to educational policy and practice in the future. These flaws can be divided into three clear categories. The first concerns the interpretative paradigm of educational research. This tends to involve small-scale case-study research that relies on qualitative analysis. The second category concerns the positivist paradigm. This tends to involve experiments or quasi-experiments, psychometrics and quantitative analysis. The third concerns the ways in which research into peer mediation tends to be conceptualized, and the flawed assumptions that underlie much of the research in this area, whether it involves an interpretative or a positivist paradigm. The chapter will end with some suggestions for research in the future which might begin to find ways around some of these difficulties.

Interpretativist research into peer mediation

Research into the effectiveness of peer mediation tends to be grounded in an interpretative paradigm. It is generally carried out by participant researchers, often using action research, or by project workers who have developed peer mediation in a school, or group of schools. Some of it is carried out by individuals or teams who have financial or professional interests in the ongoing success of peer mediation (the author included). This is not to suggest that issues of rigour and objectivity feature to any greater extent in research into peer mediation than in research into any other area of education; it is merely to suggest that this research is not immune from the same dilemmas and ethical issues that face a good deal of research in the social sciences.

Evaluations of peer mediation programmes are usually positive. Much of this research has been carried out in the US. For example, Gentry and Benenson (1993) found that 27 grade four to six 'conflict managers' experienced a decline in the frequency and intensity of conflicts with siblings as a result of peer mediation training at school, and that parents perceived a similar decline in the frequency of such conflicts and in their need to intervene. Crary (1992) evaluated the effects of a peer mediation programme conducted in a large, culturally diverse, urban middle school. He found that all of the 125 disputants who used the service managed to resolve their conflicts and were satisfied with the outcomes. Teachers also indicated that the amount of conflict in school was lowered. Miller (1993) describes a Maryland middle school that initiated a peer mediation programme in response to increasing numbers of fights. She found that after one year both the number of suspensions given by teachers, and student arguments observed in school, decreased. School climate and the quality of student relationships improved, and many students used the mediation process both within and outside of school. Thompson (1996) and Rogers (1996) also report positive results for the use of a peer mediation programme.

Research into a peer mediation programme that is typical of much of this research in the US was carried out by Araki (1990). Peer mediation services were set up in a school complex in the Honolulu district of Hawaii by the Dispute Management Schools Project (DMSP). The school complex was made up of a high school, one of its feeder intermediate schools and one of its feeder elementary schools. The programme was initiated because Araki, the project manager, felt that a serious 'frustration gap' existed between the students' expectations of being involved in decisions affecting them and the extent to which they really were. The programme aimed to enable students to participate in the resolution of their own disputes giving them a greater sense of ownership.

The evaluation of this programme showed that an experienced and committed project coordinator was felt to be essential, as were additional resources. The full-time coordinator of this project had a wide range of roles. The most important of these were conducting the startup activities; orientating the staff to the programme; training the staff and student mediators; ensuring that the intake, execution and followup of the mediation service was executed effectively; and maintaining the profile of the project, not only at school level but also at district and state levels. The evaluation also revealed that communicating regularly with staff and parents about the project was essential to its success, as were ongoing training for the mediators and adapting the programme to fit in with other areas of school life.

The volunteer student mediators, who were identified as 'perceived leaders', completed a training programme of 20 hours. They were required to be on call to mediate throughout the school day, to agree to make up any schoolwork missed and to behave in a mature and supportive manner throughout the training and implementation of the programme. The mediators demonstrated more positive attitudes and improved academic performance and feelings of empowerment following the programme. Disputants who had used the service also demonstrated these improvements in attitude. A total of 136 cases were mediated between 1986 and 1988. Twelve of these were teacher-student disputes, mediated by a teacher and a student, and the rest were student-student disputes, mediated by two students. Overall, there was a 92.6 per cent success rate. The project coordinator and school counsellors identified the characteristics of an effective mediator as someone who: is confident; has a good understanding of the mediation process; is able to write agreements clearly; has leadership abilities (but not the same as a student councillor or representative); is directive; is responsible; is caring; is a good listener and knows how to ask questions. Many disputants were identified as being non-listeners who had a history of conflicts and poor problem-solving skills. They were also not usually involved with extracurricular activities.

Significantly more females than males participated in the programme as disputants, and there was a correlation between gender and types of conflict that came to mediation. Overall, there were eight major categories of conflict addressed: gossip/rumour, arguments, dirty looks, poor classroom behaviour, harassment, jealousy, fights and invasion of privacy. The three highest types of conflict experienced by females were gossip/rumour, arguments and harassment, and the most noticeable type of conflict experienced by males was harassment. The highest proportion of disputes was found to occur among students in grade eight (11-to-12-year-olds). The conflicts occurring most frequently at high school level were arguments, with gossip/rumour occurring most frequently at intermediate school level and harassment at elementary level. The mediation process was not found to be more or less successful with any particular ethnic group.

Difficulties encountered by the project organizers included a lack of ongoing experience-based training for the mediators and a limited number of cases relative to the numbers of mediators trained – which meant that they were unable to sharpen their skills. Whether or not mediation was used was dependent on the extent to which adults in school were supportive of the project, and in particular on teachers' willingness to release students from class for mediation. Scheduling mediation sessions at the convenience of all parties was a major problem. Araki concludes that the DMSP was largely successful.

Johnson and Johnson (1996) have carried out a meta-analysis of a many pieces of research into peer mediation. They found that, overall, 85 to 95 per cent of disputes mediated by peers result in lasting and stable agreements. Students trained in mediation tended to engage in less antisocial and more prosocial behaviour in school, and violence and other serious discipline problems decreased. On average, referrals to the principal were reduced by 60 per cent. Generally, the most frequent conflicts were found by Johnson and Johnson to result from gossip/rumour, harassment, arguments, threats of physical violence and negative behaviour in the classroom. Johnson and Johnson go on to strike a note of caution, however, warning that most of these studies were of poor quality methodologically.

In New Zealand, staff from 12 Auckland schools who set up peer mediation programmes describe the changes that they saw (Duncan, 1993):

> 'I don't have so many children rushing up to me on duty.'
> 'I often hear the children say, "let's find the mediators, they'll help."'
> 'Incidents have lessened in the playground, children are much more responsible.'
> 'Mediators take their job seriously and excellent training has helped them to "solve" many types of problems. I am impressed with how they handle situations. I have not yet had to step in.'

One of the principals of the schools describes the concerns that led him to initiate a peer mediation programme. 'My concern was always that the children's problems were not being addressed at earlier stages, and occasionally incidents of "bullying" would emerge which could have been caught if the child concerned had someone to take that problem to other than a duty teacher' (Duncan, 1993: 2). After the peer mediation service was implemented, he notes a change:

> The difference as I see it is that children, particularly the younger ones, feel more secure in the playground. They now know where to take their problems and be heard. My deputy principal follows through the reports and discusses any patterns or concerns arising. These days the discussions are few and far between as the incidents are becoming minor. The older children have learned skills to empower them to deal with their peers. Therefore I have my schedule back!
> (Duncan, 1993: 3)

Southwark Mediation Centre in London reported on their project to develop peer mediation programmes in three local secondary schools (Southwark Mediation Centre, 1993). The project coordinator gives an example of a successfully mediated dispute:

> In one dispute, insults such as 'slag' 'bitch,' etc. had been regularly exchanged and the whole class had become involved. Feelings in the mediation session became very heated, but the mediators were successful in bringing down the temperature and getting the two sides to talk calmly to each other. At the end, both girls said 'thank-you' to the mediators and they have since become friends. One of the

mediators said of this case: 'getting this problem resolved made me feel really good'.

> (Southwark Mediation Centre, 1993: 14)

The school counsellor who was responsible for the peer mediation programme in one of the schools says of the programme:

> I have seen that the teaching of mediation skills begins to alter young people's attitudes and the way in which they conduct themselves. This is an exciting project because it puts the responsibility back to the students and they have shown they are willing to take it. They will respond more to each other and it is very valuable that they, rather than adults, will be doing the mediation. It also develops respect for other people's viewpoints and can address the many serious and highly disruptive conflicts in the school. It makes it possible for these conflicts to be resolved by thinking and not by fighting.
>
> (Southwark Mediation Centre, 1993: 14)

Tyrrell and Farrell (1995) used action research to evaluate peer mediation programmes in two primary schools in Northern Ireland. The research involved interviews with students, teachers, and other adults in school, and student questionnaires. At the end of the first year they made a number of recommendations based on their research findings. These are that peer mediation should be established in Northern Ireland schools and that resources should be developed for a Northern Irish context. They also concluded that as many children as possible should be trained in each school, that appropriate procedures should be developed for the selection of those who will function as mediators, and that those not selected should have complementary functions in the service's provision. They equally stress the importance of research and of ensuring that schools are clear from the outset about their role in assisting this research.

Teachers from Birmingham (UK) evaluated peer mediation equally favourably. Stacey and Robinson (1997) give a number of examples of teacher and student evaluations of peer mediation projects in Birmingham. The behaviour coordinator of a Birmingham primary school says:

> Mediation began as an aspect of school life, a taught element, and has become something which they use as part of their everyday lives, as useful as language and maths. Their skills, at whatever level, have extended into their homes and lives outside school.
>
> (Stacey and Robinson, 1997)

The headteacher of the school adds:

We were looking for ways to further enhance our behaviour policy when we first became involved with mediation ... Our first mediators were brilliant. It was wonderful to watch them grow in confidence as the scheme got underway and was successful. Our third group of mediators has just started. The children never fail to amaze us. They get better every year ... The whole process of mediation has made a huge difference to our school. We find it almost impossible to say exactly why it has worked so well. It is a combination of many things. Perhaps the most important is that we did it as a whole school. I can't imagine our school without mediation. We feel really proud of what our children have achieved using the process of mediation.

(Stacey and Robinson, 1997: 158)

The head of year seven at a Birmingham secondary school states:

The peer mediation process has proved to be a valuable tool since it began seven months ago. The skills taught to all of the students have helped to create a positive and pleasant atmosphere within classrooms and around the school. The chosen mediators themselves have grown in stature, assuming responsibility for operating the scheme. Their mature approach has been appreciated by disputants and their success has certainly eased my pastoral workload.

(Stacey and Robinson, 1997: 158)

These quotes from people who have had direct experience of peer mediation show that it is certainly perceived to be of value. Of particular interest to teachers are the often-repeated advantages for the mediators themselves and the positive effect peer mediation appears to have on the quality of life in school. Some caution does, however, need to be exercised in interpreting the results from these studies. It is perhaps to be expected that teachers or headteachers who invest significant time in introducing peer mediation into their school will be particularly receptive to findings and anecdotes that reinforce that this time was well spent. This is especially the case if peer mediation is introduced because it ties in with a teacher's strongly held beliefs about the nature of power and schooling. Charity workers, project managers and academics with a specialism in this field have just as many professional interests tied up with the success of peer mediation. In some cases, these interests are also financial, with ongoing funding dependent on successful outcomes against measurable targets.

Special bonds can be established between busy teachers, who can feel isolated in their classrooms, and peer mediation project workers who come in regularly to engage in a shared project. Project workers are often hungry for examples of how their work is having an impact on the students (as are the charitable or state-sector organizations that employ them) and teachers are usually happy to oblige. The 'feel-good factor' of peer mediation, especially in the early days, is very strong and this can be reinforcing for adults and children alike. Less reinforcing and often ignored, are the times when peer mediation could have been used, but wasn't, the times when it is tedious or inappropriate, the times when no one turns up to unlock the room, and the times when teachers revert back to authoritarian methods of resolving disputes because they are tired, stressed, or just because they can. More research is needed into the longitudinal effects of peer mediation. Lyon (1991) for example, describes how, in an inner-city middle school, the positive effects of a peer mediation service were lost when the programme ceased to function. She concludes that, to be successful in reducing disputes, interventions must be long term and consistently available. More ethnographic research is also needed in order to better understand the complex processes that occur in a school when some aspects of power are equalized through mediation.

Education is not the only area to experience problems in establishing a strong research base for mediation. Research into mediation (and ADR more generally) is characterized by discussion of methods and techniques with little regard for the development of theory or research methodology. This applies across work in law, sociology, education and psychology. Mack's (2003) comprehensive review, for example, of research studies relating to the optimal time for court and tribunal referral to ADR failed to produce any generalized checklist guidance of relevant criteria and indeed specifically advised against attempting any such exercise. Despite reporting some positive and consistent messages from the research (for example, the regular results of high client satisfaction with mediation) the review concluded there were substantial limits on the ability of empirical research to establish clear referral criteria.

Positivist research into peer mediation

Problems associated with research into peer mediation are not restricted to small-scale case-study designs, however. Larger scale experimental or quasi-experimental test-retest designs can also hit difficulties associated with a lack of sensitivity and flexibility. Stuart (1991), for example, is one of the few researchers into peer mediation to use quantitative data analysis. She used interviews and questionnaires to evaluate a 'conflict manager' programme developed for third to fifth grade students in an elementary school in Virginia. The results showed that the programme reduced tension, enhanced student self-esteem, increased student levels of responsibility, increased the teaching time for staff, and improved students' problem-solving, communication, cooperation, and critical thinking skills. What is not clear, however, is the interface between the data collection and the statistical analysis. At the basis of this research are young people and adults completing questionnaires and participating in interviews, with all of the opportunities for bias already explored. The application of statistical analysis is not sufficient in itself to mitigate against these effects.

Positivist experimental or quasi-experimental designs attempt to eliminate subjectivity through measuring data that can be easily quantified, and through scaling up in order to reduce the effects of anomalies. All of this is covered by statistical analysis, which will give a numerical indication of significance. It is possible, it is claimed, to indicate real change (or lack of it) regardless of the proclivities of the people involved. Much of the experimental and quasi-experimental research into peer mediation that has been carried out to date has used quantitative data such as levels of bullying, levels of violence in school, student self-esteem and student locus of control. The first two tend to use questionnaires based on checklists of particular kinds of behaviour experienced by victims, witnesses or perpetrators, and the second two tend to use questionnaires based on psychometrics. Difficulties with questionnaires based on checklists will be explored later in this chapter but it is worth pausing briefly here in order to critique the use of psychometrics in programme evaluation.

Perhaps the most common psychometric measure used to evaluate programmes of various kinds is self esteem. Emler (2001) however, has pointed out that using the self-esteem in this way is deeply flawed. William James (1890) first brought the self out of the realms of philosophy and defined it as a legitimate study for the psychologist. Since Freud, a number of psychologists (notably Rogers, 1951 and Maslow, 1962) have developed the concept of self-esteem. Diggory (1966) and other social psychologists, made it a common subject of study. The self (or self concept) was seen (for example, by Rogers, 1951) to be made up of three components: self image, self esteem and ideal self. The self image and the ideal self are seen as descriptive concepts, referring to the kind of person the individual thinks he or she is, or would like to be. Self esteem is seen as essentially evaluative, referring to the extent to which the individual likes or accepts him or herself. According to this formula, an individual's self esteem will be high if they experience a high degree of acceptance from others, and low if they feel judged or required to be different. Coppersmith (1967) has defined self esteem as a personal judgement of worthiness, expressed in the attitudes the individual holds towards himself/ herself. Lawrence (1981) – whose definition grew out of his clinical counselling work with eight-to-11-year-olds – has defined it as the child's affective evaluation of the sum total of his or her characteristics both mental and physical. It is Lawrence's LAWSEQ questionnaire that has been most commonly used in measuring children's self esteem.

The difficulty with the concept of self esteem is that, technically, it is morally neutral, although this is not the way in which it is often used. For example, if a young person's ideal self can steal cars without getting caught, and s/he is able to do this, then s/he will have high self esteem. This is not what is usually meant by social workers, teachers and psychologists talking about self-esteem, however – in fact, quite the reverse. Such a young person would be seen as having low self esteem, and as being in need of intervention to achieve greater self worth and reduced antisocial behaviour. So what then is really meant by self esteem? When well-meaning professionals talk about raising self-esteem (usually of working-class boys, often black) perhaps what they really mean is making them more like 'us'. One could even go further to suggest that middle-class people hold working-class young people in low esteem. One could suggest that in order to avoid uncomfortable feelings associated with elitism or racism, such well-meaning professionals might subconsciously find a way of locating low esteem within working-class young people themselves – so that it is they (not us) who hold themselves in low esteem. They are the source of their own problems. Psychologists talk about this process as reaction formation. Social problems, the story goes, are solved, not by middle-class people living more ethical and socially responsible lives, but by working-class people learning to 'love themselves' more. It is the 'leg up' version of social change, in which teachers, counsellors, volunteers, project workers and so forth maintain their self-image as caring supportive people, whilst benefiting from processes of social exclusion.

Emler (2001) in a report into self-esteem commissioned by the Joseph Rowntree Foundation criticizes 'conceptual entrepreneurs' for their role in creating a market for all kinds of initiatives that are purported to increase self esteem alongside a number of other social benefits. He cautions that, 'High self esteem is ... very unlikely to be the all-purpose social vaccine that some have supposed it to be' (Emler, 2001: 59). In a meta-analysis of research into such initiatives, he found that, despite millions of pounds of government money being spent, no link could be found between low self esteem and antisocial or destructive behaviour. In fact, the only link that he did find was between high self esteem and certain males who commit violent acts. One of the clearer messages of the research that he reviewed was that self esteem remains surprisingly stable, with people deploying a range of strategies to discount any evidence that contradicts the opinions they have of themselves. There seems little benefit, therefore, in using self esteem as a measure of the effectiveness of peer mediation. He concludes:

> The most important influences on a person's level of self-esteem are their parents. This influence is partly genetic and partly produced by the degree of love, concern, acceptance and interest shown by parents through childhood and adolescence. Physical and particularly sexual abuse by parents has especially damaging and enduring

> effects. It also seems that after parents have had their say little else in
> life will be able to modify the opinion of self thus formed.
>
> (Emler, 2001: 59)

Others have attempted to use observation in order to improve objectivity and rigour. Another large-scale evaluation of a peer mediation programme was carried out by Johnson et al. (1994). They found that 92 first- to sixth-grade students, in four multi-age classes in an American suburban elementary school, were able to transfer procedures and skills from a peer-mediation training programme to their own peer conflicts. Prior to the training programme, which took place over six weeks for 30 minutes a day, frequent conflicts involving academic work, physical aggression, playground activities, possession of objects, turn taking, put downs and teasing were reported. Careful observation of hallways, the dining room, the playground and the gymnasium revealed that four months after the training, students seriously and carefully used their training to resolve highly emotional and prolonged conflicts with their peers. The frequency of student-student conflicts that teachers needed to manage dropped by 80 per cent after the training, and the number of conflicts referred to the principal was reduced to zero.

To determine how well they had learned to negotiate and mediate students were videotaped negotiating a resolution of two conflicts immediately after the training, and six months later. They were also given a questionnaire in which conflicts were described and students were asked to write down how they would mediate. The results demonstrated that the students knew the mediation process and were able to apply it. Many of the students and their parents reported that they were using the negotiation and mediation skills at home with their siblings, family, and friends. The use of videotape and observation here are intended to add rigour to the design, although it could be argued that observers in classrooms and corridors will always alter the dynamics of conflict and that it is not surprising that children will know how to mediate better when they have been taught how to do it.

Returning to my research evaluating peer mediation in three Birmingham primary schools, it will be recalled that a quasi-experiment was chosen in order to attempt to reduce the effects of bias due to my ongoing professional interests in peer-mediation. In practice, the choice of this method created as many problems as it solved. Results showed that, in School One (the only school in which the full peer mediation project was followed through) changes in the dependent variable of bullying did occur during the period of the research, although not in ways that were predicted (see Tables 8.1 and 8.2). The actual practice of peer mediation had more effect on reducing bullying than the peer mediation training. Indeed, the peer mediation training coincided with (non-significant) increases in bullying others in

Table 8.1 Numbers of students experiencing changes in frequency of being bullied over the three times of testing in School One and the Control School

		Baseline to post-training	Post-training to post-peer mediation service	Baseline to post-peer mediation service
School One	Reduction in being bullied	16	15 ↓	25 ↓
	Increase in being bullied	16	5	15
	No change	24	36	16
Control School	Reduction in being bullied	8	2	7
	Increase in being bullied	3	2	3
	No change	9	16	10

Table 8.2 Numbers of students changing the frequency of bullying others over the three times of testing in School One and the Control School

		Baseline to post-training	Post-training to post-peer mediation service	Baseline to post-peer mediation service
School One	Reduction in bullying others	6	17 ↓	14
	Increase in bullying others	17	6	11
	No change	33	33	31
Control School	Reduction in bullying others	2	2	1
	Increase in bullying others	3	3	3
	No change	15	15	16

School One. In Table 8.1 and Table 8.2, significant change is indicated by an arrow. More information about the research design is given in Chapter One.

Threats to the validity of quasi-experimental research designs have been identified by Cook et al. (1990) as: statistical conclusion validity; internal validity; construct validity; and external validity. Threats to internal validity that are particularly relevant here include those relating to 'testing' and 'history'. Student questionnaires to test for levels of bullying can only ever measure the extent to which students are conscious of their behaviour and experiences, and/or the extent to which they are able to admit to it, even in the form of an anonymous questionnaire (Cook et al.'s 'evaluation apprehension'). Clearly the amount of bullying reported by students can be influenced by their awareness of what bullying is, and antibullying curriculum work can result in the problem of bullying appearing to grow before it can get better. This issue has also been encountered by Smith (DfEE, 1994) in his review of antibullying initiatives carried out on behalf of the DfES.

In a similar vein, over the 18-month experimental period, some of the change (or apparent lack of it) in the nature and frequency of bullying recorded in the teacher interviews, may have been due to changing teacher perceptions. Some reductions in students' experiences of being bullied may have been missed by teachers who were increasingly aware of bullying, especially the more subtle forms of psychological bullying. This implies a basic flaw in experiments that use a reduction in bullying as the only measure of the success of peer mediation programmes.

The 'history' threat, where the presumed relationship between the cause and effect might be due to some unrelated event taking place between the pretest and the post-test, was significant here, because the intervention of peer mediation took place over 18 months, during which time a wide variety of other events occurred in the experimental and control classrooms. Although the control school did partially enable some standardization of this effect, it is nevertheless clear that a whole range of factors could have been responsible for the changes that occurred in School One and in the control school. Indeed, an issue for research into peer mediation and bullying is the difficulty in managing variables in control settings. If one accepts, for example, that it is the aim of any teacher in any school to reduce bullying and improve peer relationships amongst students, then one must also accept the difficulty in establishing a true control setting for research into bullying and peer mediation in a school. There is a real challenge in persuading teachers in control situations to withhold from using methods with their classes that may interfere with the experiment, especially when the teachers involved believe that these methods will help them to achieve their own objectives for their class.

Care was taken, here, to minimize the effects of these threats, but the difficulty of using an 'agricultural-botanical' paradigm for research into peer mediation soon became apparent (Stenhouse, 1987). These threats have been encountered elsewhere (DfEE, 1994) and do not, in themselves, negate the use of quasi-experimental research designs to evaluate educational interventions. They do, however, highlight the difficulty of carrying out experiments in a school setting. Standardization was weak due to the fact that the teachers were working in different environments with differing levels of skill and experience, and the two schools that did not follow the program to the end seriously jeopardized the main experiment.

For future research into peer mediation, perhaps Parlett and Hamilton's (1972) concept of 'illuminative evaluation' could be useful. With illuminative evaluation, observation, interviews with participants (students, instructors, administrators and others), questionnaires, and analysis of documents and background information are all combined to help 'illuminate' problems, issues, and significant programme features. Parlett and Hamilton suggest that this is a particularly apposite research tool for the evaluation of what they call 'instructional systems' of which peer mediation is an example. As they point out, an instructional system, when adopted, undergoes modifications that are rarely trivial. Although the system may remain as a shared idea and abstract model with its own terminology and shorthand, it assumes, nevertheless, a different form in every situation, which in this study means in every classroom where the programme was delivered and evaluated. They are particularly keen to point out the differences in what they call the 'learning milieu' for children in different situations who may be part of the same instructional system. The instructional system being evaluated will interact with, and cannot be separated from, the learning milieu of which it becomes part. The illuminative approach therefore has a vital role to play in illuminating any apparent differences in the data collected from each situation or classroom. In hindsight such an approach would have harmonized better with the peer mediation programme under investigation.

Conceptualizing research into peer mediation

In researching peer mediation, it is important to take into account not only the validity of the research methods used, but also of the 'fit' between the research paradigm, the dominant paradigm of the intervention being evaluated, and the social and political contexts in which the research is located. My research (reviewed above) contained a fatal flaw, which was that it used experimental methods to evaluate a humanist intervention. This research mixed positivist and humanist/interpretative paradigms with predictable results. A humanist researcher, for example, would study a programme already in place, not one imposed by the evaluator, and the programme would be evaluated through the eyes of its developers and participants, not just through the eyes of the researcher. The humanist is sceptical of standardization of social and educational interventions and doubly sceptical of any attempts to make them standard for the sake of investigation. So is the mediator!

Kyriacou and Wan Chang (1993) explore the thorny issue of whether it is possible for a single study to mix different types of data and approaches. Most researchers argue that it is possible, and indeed this is the position taken within the essentially 'eclectic' approach adopted by many researchers conducting an illuminative evaluation (Vulliamy, 1990). They argue, however, that while using both quantitative and qualitative *data* in an illuminative evaluation is acceptable; mixing research approaches is more problematic. The difficulty in mixing these two approaches concerns the fact that the interpretative research approach essentially stems from a *rejection of the positivist research* approach (Bassey, 1990). As such, a study that employs both approaches would appear to lack a coherent research stance. These are issues that have largely been neglected by researchers in the field of peer mediation.

Another issue in conceptualizing research into peer mediation in schools is connected with the way in which mediation is often seen as a means of reducing violence in schools, especially in the US. Programme evaluation (and funding) often centres around a reduction of violence in schools. This chapter will now go on to explore the nature of violence in schools and the implications of this for research into peer mediation. It questions whether methods typically used to investigate violence in schools themselves carry elements of structural violence, and ends by suggesting methods that might create greater congruence between promoting non-violence in schools and the methods used to investigate these phenomena. It could be argued that most educational research legitimizes and colludes with systems of schooling that are directly or indirectly violent, it could equally be argued that researchers investigating violence in schools and peer mediation need to take particular care in designing research that is grounded in non-violent theory and practice. Student voice, involving students as coresearchers, and the need to build capacity, democracy and citizenship within the communities investigated, is central to this.

Internationally, research into violence in schools has been growing steadily over the last decade or so (Devine, 1996; Olweus, 1999; Debarieux, 2003; Smith, 2003). There is a general perception that schools are increasingly violent places, and that both teachers and students are at risk of disruption, verbal and physical violence as they go about the daily business of teaching and learning. Most countries in the world record statistics of violent incidents involving students as perpetrators, and research investigating programmes to reduce violence in schools is widespread (Smith, 2003).

Some of these studies make alarming reading. For example, Smith (2003) reviews the levels of violence in schools in Europe. The review is based on an initiative of the European Commission under its Fifth Framework programme of research activities, and aimed to gain an overview of the situation regarding violence in schools from the 15 member states at the time, and two associated states. What follows is a brief snapshot of findings from this international comparative review.

In French secondary schools during 1999, a total of 240,000 incidents were registered with central government, with 6240 of these regarded as serious. The aggressors were mainly students, as were the victims. The next biggest group of victims was school staff. The Portuguese government

Security Cabinet saw up to 14 per cent increases in reports of violence between 1995 and 1998. In Austria, studies found that around 12 per cent of students admitted to bullying other students regularly or often (Krumm et al., 1997). In the Netherlands a nationwide random survey found that 22 per cent of students had been victims of sexual harassment by boys at least once, and 43 per cent had been a victim of intentional damage to property (Mooij, 1994). In 1995, a nationwide survey of secondary teachers in Spain was carried out at the request of Parliament and found that 72 per cent of teachers considered the lack of discipline in schools a serious problem. In the UK, the National Union of Teachers carried out a survey (Neill, 2001) which found that 83 per cent of teachers witnessed student to student violence at least once a year, and 43 per cent witnessed it on a weekly basis.

The US does not share the European preoccupation with bullying. Here the focus is more on 'dangerous schools' or 'youth gangs'. Devine and Lawson (2003) describe how so-called 'spree shootings' erupted in rural and suburban American schools in the late 1990s, ending any lingering belief that violence in schools is merely an inner-city issue. In the Columbine tragedy, two high-school students entered Columbine High School armed with two sawn-off shot guns, a semi-automatic pistol, a nine millimetre semi-automatic rifle, and over thirty pipe bombs, grenades and other explosives. They quickly killed 12 students and a teacher. They also wounded 23 others before taking their own lives.

The response to this perceived increase in violence in schools is a whole raft of programmes and measures designed to reduce violence amongst students, and attacks on teachers. From Italy to Spain to Germany to the US intervention programmes are being funded by governments who wish to be seen to be addressing these ills. Educational programmes against school violence have been grouped into four categories: programmes aimed at innovation or changes in the organization of the school; programmes aimed at teacher training; proposals for classroom activities and educational programmes for dealing with school violence (Ortega et al., 2003).

But are indiscipline, bullying and student-to-student violence really endemic in schools internationally? Are these state funds well spent? Reviewing the European research quoted earlier (which is mainly based on self-report) Smith (2003) notes that, 'It is not clear that violence is getting worse but many people perceive it as getting worse.' This perception is fuelled by the media, as the contributors from Portugal in Smith (2003) point out, 'the excessive media attention, and the use of school violence as a political argument, makes the phenomenon appear larger than it really is and contributes to the growing feeling of insecurity, which is not really supported by data' (Sebastiao et al., 2003). In France, according to the same statistics quoted earlier, there are lower rates of violence in schools than in society in general. School is thus one of the safest places to be.

Perhaps there are three issues that need to be addressed in order to get nearer to the truth. One is the question of whether school students are more violent than the rest of the population. The second is whether adults in schools perpetuate violence against young people, and the third is the extent to which structural violence is endemic in the process of schooling. If these matters can be better understood, then responses to violence (including peer mediation) can be better tailored to meet the needs of students, parents, teachers and the local, national and international communities to which they belong.

Although there has been a tenfold increase in reported violent crime in the UK since 1979, Gilbert (2006) builds a case for his assertion that 'yobbery' has become not just a problem of the young and the poor – the whole of society has become coarser and more violent – following his journey throughout the UK interviewing both the perpetrators and the victims of violence, aggression and antisocial behaviour. As reported in Chapter Three, he gives graphic accounts of violence, bullying and humiliation in the senior ranks of the army, the media, the city, international banks and political parties. Perhaps young people in schools merely reflect societal trends in general. If this is indeed the case, then care needs to be taken before buying into interventions and programmes which claim to have the facility to make schools better than the rest of the society. Discourses which view teachers as non-violent implementers of programmes aimed at violent students neglect the reality that teachers are just as implicated in the reproduction of violent norms as anyone else.

Harber (2004) claims that schools have always sanctioned and legitimized direct violence against children. Corporal punishment in schools is still regularly used in between one-third and half of all countries in the world. At the end of the 1990s corporal punishment was still widely used and approved of in the US, and was legal in 27 out of 50 states. Harber gives examples of the role of schooling in directly contributing to hatred of other groups. He shows how education systems and schools have actively encouraged separation, prejudice and discrimination against minority groups, or been directly implicated in violence on the basis of inter-group hatred, in countries such as Bosnia, Cyprus, Germany, India, Herzegovina, Kosovo, Sri Lanka, Israel, Palestine and Rwanda. In the Rwandan genocide of 1994, when up to a million people were murdered in the space of a few weeks, teachers from a Hutu ethnic background commonly denounced their Tutsi students to the militia or even killed them themselves.

There are also many instances of violence in schools through direct or indirect racism, sexism, and homophobia, and through omission in some countries, where a lack of adequate education against HIV/AIDS results in the death of students. Harber links schooling with sexual abuse, and gives examples from sub-Saharan Africa and from Ireland, Britain and Japan. In

Japan reports of sexual misconduct by teachers in schools rose tenfold between 1989 and 2000. A South African Medical Research Council survey carried out in 1998 found that among those rape victims who specified their relationship to the perpetrator, 37.7 per cent said their school teacher or principal had raped them (Human Rights Watch, 2001). Besag (2006) shows how schools in the UK often do nothing about the misery caused by girls' bullying, as it can be subtle and hard to tackle.

These matters cannot be ignored when considering student-to-student or student-to-teacher violence in schools. Perhaps human weakness is more visible in children than in adults. Providing remedial programmes for children may be more palatable than engaging with shameful adult behaviour. Discourses where children are seen as sources of hope and optimism, and where redemption for adults is somehow tied in with keeping violence at the school boundaries – as if security fences and CCTV cameras could keep the badness out – are comforting, but inadequate.

Arguments about the inherently alienating, authoritarian and oppressive nature of schooling are not new (Holt, 1969; Illich, 1971; Freire, 1972), but few have gone so far as to suggest that schooling itself is violent or harmful. Harber (2004) argues that concern with schooling globally has focused on the *right to* education, rather than on *rights in* education, and that organizations such as UNESCO have ignored the fact that: 'Learning can either be very good or bad depending on what is learnt, how it is learnt and what it is designed to do'. One explanation for the low levels of enrolment and retention in schooling in developing countries could be that it is of poor quality and even harmful.

Resistance amongst parents in these countries may be far more rational and informed than is widely believed. African schools, for example, have been characterized by hierarchical organization, rote learning and teacher-centred classrooms (Fuller, 1991). In South America, where 'frontal teaching' is the norm, half of those that start school drop out before finishing primary school. Harber quotes Green (1998) who claims that four out of five Chilean teachers merely dictate classes to their students, who sit passively in rows. In the UK a recent survey of how the national curriculum was implemented over a five year period (involving 7,000 students, 250 teachers and the observation of 97 lessons) concluded that it led to the rote-learning of subject-specific knowledge so that students may perform well in written tests of memory (Griffith, 2000). French classrooms have been characterized as 'catechistic' and having a didactic highly authoritarian teaching style with an emphasis on the product more than on the process of learning (Broadfoot, 1999). As discussed in earlier chapters, neoliberalism and neoconservatism in schools contribute to a climate in which student perspectives are marginalized and authoritarian models of behaviour management in schools lead to the reproduction, not only of the socio-economic and political inequalities of the surrounding society, but also of the violent relationships and systems of control and surveillance that often go with them.

Viewed in this way, it soon becomes evident that there is a need to question some of the assumptions inherent in research into peer mediation, which ignores the wider context of violence in schools. It is important to question the aims and methods of research, which, perhaps unintentionally, serves to legitimize or collude with violent or oppressive systems of schooling. Some educationalists have begun to respond to these dilemmas, for example through the reflective teaching movement (Stenhouse, 1975; Schon, 1991) and 'critical theory,' a root of practitioner research in education. 'Liberatory education' 'emancipatory education' or critical pedagogy, derived from the liberationist philosophies of Freire (1972) also aim to think critically in order to recognize the ways in which dominant ideologies and social structures work at coercing and oppressing.

These more critical stances place the teacher and researcher at the centre of the research process. They also take account of the ways in which teachers and researchers (re)construct oppressive policy and practice, and discourses of violence in classrooms, while investigating and seeking to disrupt them. Researchers are not neutral observers – they are inextricably linked with the various communities that form their identities. They cannot separate themselves out for the purpose of research. What is more, teachers and researchers hold privilege and power that students are not able to access, and this leads to a certain quality of relation that predetermines the outcomes of research. Taking account of this, researchers could pose themselves more far-reaching questions. Examples of questions (adapted from Brown and Jones, 2001) that could be used to inform a more ethical and effective approach to researching peer mediation and violence in schools include:

- How can the researcher observe violence in schools without being implicated in it?
- In constructing validity criteria for our assertions, whose interests are we serving?
- What counts as development towards less violent schooling?
- Whose voices matter in researching violence in schools?

Box 8.1 contains a proposal for carrying out non-violent research into citizenship education. This proposal involves students as active agents in the research process. The laboratory schools research proposal aims to involve young people in enhancing democratic processes in their schools while engaging in reflexive practice. In this way it aims to ensure congruity between the aims and values of citizenship education and the research stance adopted. Young people are involved in the research process from inception through to dissemination, and their voices are an integral part of the *process* of the research, and not just the content. They form part of the research project steering group, and take their place alongside adult coresearchers to determine the areas to be investigated, the methods to be adopted, and the budget allocations. This is predicated on training and support for these young researchers, and facilitation of meetings, where necessary, to ensure an equal distribution of power and voice.

Box 8.1 *The Citizenship Laboratory School research proposal*

Research aims

- To improve the quality of citizenship education in schools through innovation, research and engagement with the voice of the child.
- To ensure that young people are involved in the research process as active agents from inception through to dissemination.
- To ensure congruity between the aims and values of citizenship education and the research stance adopted.

Research objectives

- Via the promotion of *laboratory schools*, to further notions of critical dialogic research between academics, teachers and students as they share in the process of developing and using research.
- To use this research project to develop practical models for exchange and collaboration between academics, teachers and students.
- To strengthen links between research, policy development, reflective practice and innovation in citizenship classrooms.
- To enhance young people's research skills, thus increasing their educational and social capital.

Research outcomes

1. The establishment of a small number of *laboratory schools*, within which focused research and streamlined liaison between university and school is able to occur in the area of citizenship education.
2. Development within the *laboratory schools*, resulting from teacher and student-initiated inquiries into citizenship education.
3. Dissemination of research findings in accordance with methods selected by the research project steering group. These may include:

    - writeups of the research undertaken in professional and academic journals with key recommendations for both citizenship education, and for working with young people as coresearchers;
    - a national conference at the end of the project, run in conjunction with key citizenship organizations, to disseminate findings and recommendations;

- an annual citizenship conference organized by students in the citizenship *laboratory schools* for students from schools elsewhere in their local authority;
- a project Web site produced by students and teachers in the citizenship *laboratory schools* to support others engaged in a similar process of research and innovation.

4. Liaison and exchange between citizenship *laboratory schools*.

Project management

The research project will be managed by a project steering group. This will be made up of one or two experts in citizenship education, headteachers from the laboratory schools (or their representatives), students from each school and academics. Each school will have a steering group which will manage the project in their school in accordance with the wider aims of the project steering group. The school steering groups will be made up of the headteacher, the citizenship subject leader, a community representative or parent, an academic and five students.

Research activity

Activity will be centred around two different, but complimentary, foci – these being school-initiated research and project-initiated research. Research activity within both of these foci will be stimulated, developed and evaluated by the steering groups. Interaction between the schoolteachers, students, academics and experts participating in the project will be supported through facilitation and training where necessary, to ensure that all voices are given equal and appropriate status. Project-initiated research will take account of national and international trends that are of interest to all of the participating schools, and will include an element of comparative analysis across laboratory schools. School-initiated research will take account of emerging needs and interests from the school-based process of audit and review, and will be different in each school.

Once the steering groups have identified areas for investigation, they will design and resource the research against an annual budget. Key to any research design is the involvement of young people as researchers, and training will need to be provided to ensure that this can happen. One possible way of working would be for students and research assistants to pair up as 'buddies'. It is important to reiterate that the nature of potential projects cannot be prescribed, given the priority of schools' own analyses of issues for investigation. However, one might predict that data would come from a variety of sources, such as:

- school ethos questionnaires;
- individual and focus group interviews;
- interviews with members of the school council (facilitated by older students);
- interviews with disaffected/excluded students (facilitated by older students) and their parents;
- existing school documentation (public and general);

- existing school documentation relating to citizenship, including policy documents and schemes of work;
- observation of citizenship lessons.

Box 8.2 contains a proposal for engaging student mediators in international comparative research. The aim here is to develop research methodology for investigating peer mediation that has congruence with its humanistic underpinnings, and that locates peer mediators as subjects, rather than objects, of research by involving them in the research project as reflexive active agents.

The approach being advocated here responds to the complexity of violence in schools, with all its many facets, and enables adults and students in school to engage in a dialogic and reflexive process of cross-national review and exchange. It is anticipated that these processes would bring about changes and improvements in policy and practice for peer mediation in these schools, but the focus of these changes has not been mandated *a priori* by powerful teachers and researchers. The young people themselves have much to contribute here, and also much to gain from engaging in a far-reaching and meaningful debate with adults and peers from different countries, and from training and support in educational research methodology. Evidence of young people's capacities to engage with this kind of research is provided by the Learning School project (MacBeathe and Sugimine, 2003). Three successive groups of young people aged between 16 and 18 spent 12 months visiting and evaluating secondary schools in eight participating countries. After being trained in basic research methods, they spent up to six weeks looking at each of eight secondary schools – one from each country. What they achieved, intellectually, socially and personally, was remarkable (Ruddock and Flutter, 2004).

Box 8.2   *Peer mediation in schools: research proposal for an international comparative analysis*

Research aims

- To investigate, compare and contrast processes of peer mediation in schools in three different countries.
- To develop research methodology for investigating peer mediation that has congruence with its humanistic underpinnings.
- To investigate the impact of culture (school, community and national) on the practice of peer mediation.
- To investigate the effect of introducing an international comparative perspective on peer mediators and teachers.
- To locate peer mediators as subjects, rather than objects, of research by involving them in the research project as reflexive active agents.

Research outline

1. Research teams are established in three countries. They set up a means of communicating using online discussion.
2. Researchers from all three countries meet up to finalize the research agenda. Methods for training young people as researchers are agreed.
3. In each country the research teams set up a research project steering group, which is based on collaboration between a university, a local authority, and a community mediation service.
4. Each national research project steering group selects a school to participate. Criteria for selection include:

   - peer mediation has been established for at least two years, and there is senior management and teacher/coordinator support;
   - students have received extensive training and ongoing support;
   - peer mediator services are being accessed by fellow students on a regular basis.

5. Students and teachers from the schools join the national research project steering groups. At least half of the steering group is now made up of young people. All members of the steering groups have access to the international on-line discussion group.
6. Student mediators in each school are trained in Web design, online discussion techniques and research methods.
7. The steering groups design the research methods that will be used in the schools. These are moderated and agreed cross-nationally.
8. Each group of student mediators engages in a process of research into its mediation service. This is supported by their steering group. They publish their findings via the Web site.
9. Peer mediators and adults in each school comment on each other's Web sites using the online discussion facility that has been established.
10. These online discussions provide data that is analysed, alongside the data from the student-centred research. This process of analysis is undertaken by adult and student researchers.
11. A teacher and three student mediators from each school take part in a two-week exchange with another participating school in order to carry out ethnographic research. They reflect on the impact of the exchange on their own practice using the online discussion facility and a video diary.
12. On returning to their schools, the exchange teacher and students share their findings. They work with their steering groups to design a final stage of reflection and review in the light of international comparative perspectives.
13. Data are analysed as before and the Web site is updated.
14. A final stage of online discussion takes place. Data from this are analysed, and a final report is produced.
15. An international writing-up team, made up of adults and student mediators, meets to agree how findings will be disseminated.

Conclusion

This chapter has attempted to demonstrate that research into peer mediation, self-esteem, bullying and violence in schools is far more complex than many would suggest. Small-scale research carried out by participant researchers can be influenced by professional and financial interests, and larger scale experimental designs can be at odds with peer mediation's humanist and interpretivist underpinning. Discourses of violence and bullying in schools risk locating students as sources of violence and disruption, rather than as both perpetrators and victims alongside adults. It has suggested that those who wish to research violence in schools need to take care to avoid replicating systems and structures that are inherently damaging to students. Critical theoretical perspectives are seen here as particularly useful, as are perspectives that draw on genuine engagement with the voice of the child. Engaging in student-centred research, and ensuring a more equal distribution of power, is not presented unproblematically here, but it is suggested that involving young people as subjects, rather than objects, of research is essential for an ethical and effective response to the need to understand conflict and mediation in schools.

9 Conclusion

This book has attempted to provide an overview of policy and practice relating to peer mediation in schools, as well as key challenges that are faced by those who wish to see its use extended. In some cases these are local and financial, and in others they are conceptual and political. Whatever the challenges, it is suggested, peer mediation is a worthwhile enterprise that can result in greater empowerment and self-confidence in individuals, and greater cohesion and more peaceful environments in schools.

Mediation in general is a facilitative, non-adversarial process of dispute resolution that focuses on the needs and priorities of disputants themselves. Skilled mediators maintain neutrality, defer from making judgements and balance power between disputants. It has the power to transform conflictual relations, and to bring about long-lasting settlements in a social world that is characterized by complexity, fragmentation and individualism. Where individuals are able and willing to take responsibility for their actions, and to express genuine remorse, mediation can be seen as a valuable exercise for both the victim of a crime and the offender. Mediation in schools, where properly resourced and supported, can provide unequal opportunities for young people to engage in the vital practice of effective dispute resolution, thus improving the quality of life in school and preparing them for life beyond the school gates.

A national curriculum for citizenship that covers only traditional legal systems in the UK will not prepare young people adequately for the experiences of dispute resolution that they are likely to encounter as adults. Peer mediation, far from being a 'soft' option suitable for study as part of personal and social education, is presented here as a viable response to the need to develop more diverse, complex and globalized notions of citizenship in schools. Peace educators have long seen this link, and have been promoting peer mediation in schools for over 30 years. Peer mediation supports student-centred discipline in schools. It helps students to develop an internalized moral code and set of behavioural norms, and it helps teachers to avoid using more directive behaviour management, such as authoritarian and behaviourist methods. It is shown to be a powerful tool for inclusion of students experiencing SEBD. Failure to progress to the full implementation of peer mediation is associated with teachers remaining in control of the management of behaviour in school, and an abdication of responsibility on the part of students, who remain immature in attitude and at times difficult to control. The case studies that are presented here demonstrate that peer mediation can lead to highly successful outcomes. These include more peaceful playgrounds, enhanced skills and attainment, raised self-esteem, greater impulse control and an empowered group of learning mentors, parents and teachers. These success stories are rarer than one would hope and it is to their credit that these schools have persevered with their original vision of peaceful lunchtimes, as well as continuing to innovate and evolve.

Research into peer mediation tends to be positive. This book has attempted to demonstrate that research into peer mediation, self-esteem, bullying and violence in schools is, however, more complex than many would suggest. Small-scale research carried out by participant researchers can be influenced by professional and financial interests, and larger scale experimental designs can be at odds with peer mediation's humanist and interpretivist underpinning. Discourses of violence and bullying in schools risk locating students as sources of disruption, rather than as both perpetrators and victims of direct and indirect violence, alongside adults. It has suggested that those who wish to research violence in schools would do well to avoid replicating structures that are inherently damaging to students. Critical theoretical perspectives are seen here as particularly useful, as are perspectives that draw on genuine engagement with the voice of the child. Engaging in student-centred research, and ensuring a more equal distribution of power, is essential for the future of research into conflict and mediation in schools.

References

Abel, R. (1982) *The Politics of Informal Justice,* New York: Academic Press.

ACAS (2005) *Annual Report and Accounts,* London: The Stationery Office.

Acland, A. (1995) *Resolving disputes without going to court,* London: Century.

Antes, J.R., Folger, J.P., & Della Noce, D.J. (2001) Transforming conflict interactions in the workplace: Documented effects of the US postal service REDRESS program, *Hofstra Labor & employment law journal,* 18 (2) 429–467.

Apple, M.W. (1995) *Education and Power,* New York: Routledge.

Araki, C.T., (1990) Dispute management in the schools, *Mediation Quarterly,* 8 (1) 51–62 .

Ariès, P. (1962) *Centuries of Childhood,* London: Cape.

Astor, H. & Chinkin, C. (2001) *Dispute Resolution in Australia,* Sydney: Butterworths.

Arora, T. (1994) Measuring bullying with the Life in School checklist, *Pastoral Care in Education,* 12, 3.

Ausburger, D.W. (1992) *Conflict mediation across cultures: pathways and patterns,* Louisville: Westminster John Knox Press.

Ballard, J. (1982) *Circlebook,* New York: Irvington.

Barbalet, J. (1998) *Emotion, social theory and social structure,* Cambridge: Cambridge University Press.

Barbalet, J. (2002) *Emotions and Sociology,* Oxford: Blackwell.

Barnes, D. (1984) *From Communication to Curriculum,* London: Penguin.

Baruch Bush, R.A. & Folger, J.P. (2005) *The Promise of Mediation: The transformative approach to conflict,* San Francisco: Jossey Bass.

Bassey, M. (1990) On the Nature of Research in Education (part ii) *Research Intelligence,* No. 37, 39–44.

Beer, J. Steif, E., & Walker, C. (1987) *Peacemaking in your neighbourhood: mediator's handbook,* Friends Suburban Project, Concordville: P.A. USA.

Bell. D. (2005) *Citizenship,* Hansard Society lecture, 17 January, Accessed from http://www.ofsted.gov.uk/assets/3821.doc 6th July 2007.

Bennett, M. and Dunne, E. (1992) *Managing classroom groups,* New York: Simon and Schuster.

Berndt, T.J. (1983) Social cognition, social behaviour and children's friendships. In E.T. Higgins, D.N. Ruble & W.W Hartup (Eds.) *Social cognition and social development: A sociocultural perspective,* Cambridge: Cambridge University Press .

Berndt, T.J. (1986) Children's comments about their friendships. In M. Perimutter

(Ed.) *Cognitive perspectives on children's social and behavioural development,* Hillsdale NJ: Erlbaum.

Bernstein, B. (1977) *Class codes and control (Volume 3) Towards a theory of educational transmissions,* London: Routledge & Kegan Paul.

Besag, V. (2006) *Understanding Girl's Friendships, fights and feuds: A practical approach to girl's bullying,* Buckingham: Open University Press.

Bickmore, K. (2001) Student Conflict Resolution, Power 'Sharing' in Schools, and Citizenship Education, *Curriculum Inquiry,* 32 (2), 137—162.

Bliss, T. & Tetley, J. (1993) *Circle Time.* Bristol: Lucky Duck Publishing .

Borradori, G. (2003) *Philosophy in a time of terror: Dialogues with Jurgen Habermas and Jacques Derrida,* Chicago: University of Chicago Press.

Brace, A. (1995) Now Mediation is the Word in The War on School Violence. *The Mail on Sunday,* 19th March.

Braithwaite, J. (2001) Youth Development Circles, *Oxford Review of Education,* 27 (2) 239–252.

Brandes, D., and Ginnis, P. (1990) *The Student-Centred School,* Blackwell: Oxford.

Broadfoot, P. (1999) Comparative research on pupil achievement: in search of validity, reliability and utility. In R. Alexander, P Broadfoot & D. Philips (Eds.) *Learning from comparing,* Oxford: Symposium Books.

Brooks, L. (2006) *The story of childhood: Growing up in modern Britain,* London: Bloomsbury.

Brown, T. & Jones, L. (2001) *Action Research and Postmodernism: congruence and critique,* Buckingham: Open University Press.

Buck, T. (2005) *Administrative Justice and Alternative Dispute Resolution: the Australian experience,* Department for Constitutional Affairs, DCA Research Series 9/05, London: DCA .

Cameron, J. & Dupuis, A. (1991) The Introduction of School Mediation to New Zealand, *Journal of Research and Development in Education,* 24 (3) 1–13.

Cantor, L. (1989) Assertive discipline: More than names on the board and marbles in the jar, *Phi-Delta Kappa,* 71, 57–61.

Chitty, C. (2004) *Education policy in Britain,* Basingstoke: Palgrave.

Cohen, R. (1995) *Peer Mediation in Schools: Students Resolving Conflict.* Glenview: Goodyear Books:.

Coleman, P.T. (2000) Power and Conflict. In M. Deutsch, & P.T. Coleman (Eds.) *The Handbook of Conflict Resolution: Theory and Practice,* San Francisco: Jossey-Bass.

Community Service Volunteers (2004) *CSV reports on citizenship in the curriculum two years on,* London: CSV .

Cook, T.D., Campbell, D.T. & Perrachio, L. (1990). Quasi-experimentation. In M.D. Dunnette & L. Hough (Eds.) *Handbook of Industrial and Organizational Psychology, Second Edition, Volume I.* Palo Alto, CA: Consulting Psychologists Press.

Cook-Sather, A. (2002). Authorizing students' perspectives: Toward trust, dialogue, and change in education. *Educational Researcher*, 31 (4) 3–14.

Cooper, P. (2001) *We can work it out*, Ilford: Barnados.

Coppersmith, S. (1967) *The antecedents of self-esteem*, San Francisco: Freeman.

Cornelius, C. & Faire, S. (1989) *Everyone can win*, Sydney: Simon and Schuster.

Cowie, H. & Ruddock, J. (1988) Testing Teams, *Times Educational Supplement*, 15th April, 21.

Cowie, H. & Sharp, S. (1996) *Peer Counselling in Schools*. London: David Fulton Publishers.

Crary, D.R. (1992) Community Benefits from Mediation: A test of the "peace virus" hypothesis, *Mediation Quarterly*, 9 (3) 241–252.

Cremin (2001) An investigation into whether the 'Iceberg' system of peer mediation training, and peer mediation, reduce levels of bullying, raise self-esteem, and increase student empowerment amongst upper primary age children. Thesis available from: Leicester University, Leicester, UK.

Cremin, H. (2003) *Pupils resolving disputes: presentation of research findings from 15 English primary schools with successful peer mediation services*. Paper presented at the Second International Conference on Violence in Schools, Quebec, Canada, May 2003.

Cremin, H. & Faulks, K. (2005) *Citizenship Education Past Present and Future: Reflections from research and practice*. Paper presented at the British Educational Research Association conference, Glamorgan, September 2005.

Crick, B., (et al) (1998) *Education for citizenship and the teaching of democracy in schools: Final report of the advisory group on citizenship* (London: QCA).

Curle, A. (1981) *True Justice: Quaker peace makers and peacemaking*, London: Quaker Home Service.

Davie, R. & Galloway, D. (1996) *Listening to Children in Education*, London: David Fulton.

Davies, T. (1997) *Humanism*, London: Routledge.

Davis, G., Messmar, H., Umbreit, M., & Coates, R. (1992) *Making Amends*. London: Routledge.

de Haan, W. (1990) *The Politics of Redress*, London: Unwin Hyman.

Deakin Crick, R., Coates, M., Taylor, M. and Ritchie, S. (2004) A systematic review of the impact of citizenship education on the provision of schooling. In: *Research Evidence in Education*. London: EPPI-Centre, Social Science Research Unit, Institute of Education.

Debarbieux, E. (2003) *La violence à l'école une mondialisation*, Paper presented at the Second International Conference on Violence in Schools, Quebec City: Canada.

DEE (2002) *Inclusion in schools course book*, London: Disability Equality in Education .

Deutsch, M. (1949) A theory of cooperation and competition, *Human relations*, 2, 129–151.

Deutsch, M. (1973) *The Resolution of Conflict.* New Haven, CT: Yale University Press.

Deutsch, M. (2000) .

Deutsch, M. & Coleman, P.T. (2000) *The Handbook of Conflict Resolution: Theory and Practice,* San Francisco: Jossey-Bass.

Devine, J. (1996) *Maximum security: The culture of violence in inner city schools,* Chicago: University of Chicago Press.

Devine, J. & Lawson, H.A. (2003) The complexity of school violence: Commentary from the US, in P.K. Smith (Ed.) *Violence in schools: the response in Europe,* London: Routledgefalmer.

DES (1978) *The Warnock Report: Special Educational Needs,* London: HMSO.

DfEE (1994) *Bullying: Don't suffer in silence. An anti-bullying pack for schools.* London: HMSO.

DfES (1997) *Excellence for all children,* London: HMSO.

DfES (2004) *Working Together - giving children and young people a say,* London: HMSO .

Diggory, J.C. (1966) *Self evaluation: Concepts and studies,* New York: Wiley.

Dore, A. (1994) Miracle cure or cruel trick, *Times Educational Supplement,* March 18th 1–2.

Dubet, F. & Martucelli, D. (1996). À l' école: Sociologie de l'expérience scolaire, Paris: Seuil, coll.

Dufour, B (2006) Education for a safe world: Conflict, peace education and conflict resolution, in T. Breslin & B. Dufour (2006) *Developing citizens: A comprehensive introduction to effective citizenship education in the secondary school,* London: Hodder Murray .

Duncan, Y. (1993) *Report on Cool Schools Mediation Programme.* Available from Mediation U.K. Bristol.

Emler, N. (2001) *Self esteem: The costs and causes of low self-worth,* York: Joseph Rowntree Foundation.

ENCORE (1997) *Encore News 1997.* Available from the Education Advisor, Quaker Peace and Service, Friends House, Euston Rd., London, NW1 2BJ.

Faulks, K. (1998) *Citizenship in modern Britain,* Edinburgh: Edinburgh University Press.

Faulks, K. (2000) *Citizenship,* London: Routledge.

Fisher, P. and Ury, W. (1981) *Getting to Yes: Negotiating Agreement Without Giving In,* Boston: Houghton Mifflin.

Fiss, O. (1984) Against Settlement, *Yale Law Journal,* 93, 1073.

Fontana, D. (1994) *Managing classroom behaviour,* Leicester: BPS books.

Foucault, M. (1970) *The order of things: An archaeology of the human sciences,* London: Tavistock.

Foucault, M. (1977) *Discipline and punish: The birth of the prison,* trans. A. Sheridan, London: Allen Lane.

Fountain, S. (1999) *Peace education in UNICEF,* New York: UNICEF.

Freire, P. (1972), *Pedagogy of the Oppressed*, New York: Continuum.

Fromm, E. (1970) *The crisis of psychoanalysis: Essays on Freud, Marx and social psychology*, Middlesex: Penguin.

Fuller, B. (1991) *Growing up modern*, London: Routledge.

Garner, P. (1999) *Pupils with problems: Rational fears, Radical solutions*, Stoke: Trentham.

Gearon, L. (2003) *Learning to teach citizenship in the secondary school*, London: RoutledgeFalmer.

Gearon, L., Holness, M. & Mace, D. (2003) Learning the complexities of Citizenship, in L. Gearon (Ed.) *Learning to teach citizenship in the secondary school*, London: RoutledgeFalmer.

Genn, H. (1998) *The Central London County Court pilot mediation scheme: Evaluation report*, London: Lord Chancellor's Department.

Genn, H. (2000) *Mediation in action: Resolving court disputes without trial*, London: Calouste Gulbenkian Foundation.

Gentry, D.B., & Benenson, J.M. (1993) School to home transfer of conflict management skills among school-age children, *Families in Society*, 72 (2) 67–73.

Gilbert, F. (2006) *Yob Nation: The Truth about Britain's Yob Culture*, London: Portrait Books.

Gilligan, C. (1993) *In a different voice: Psychological theory and women's development*, London: Harvard University Press.

Glasser, C. & Roberts, S. (1993) Dispute Resolution: civil justice and its alternatives (Special Issue) *Modern Law Review* 56 (3) 277–470.

Goldthorpe, M. (1998) *Developing IEPs through Circle Time*, Cambridge: L.D.A., Wisbech.

Gray, P. (2002) *Working with Emotions: Responding to the Challenge of Difficult Pupil Behaviour in Schools*, London: Routledge.

Green, D. (1998) *Hidden lives: Voices of children in Latin America and the Caribbean*, London: Cassell.

Greenhalgh, P. (1994) *Emotional Growth and Learning*. London: Routledge .

Griffith, R. (2000) *National curriculum: national disaster?* London: RoutledgeFalmer.

Haigh, G. (1994) Blessed are the Peacemakers. *Times Educational Supplement*, 6th October, 6. .

Hall, E. & Hall, C. (1988) *Human relations in education*, London: Routledge.

Hallberlin, C.J. (2001) Transforming workplace culture through mediation: Lessons learned from swimming upstream, *Hofstra Labor & employment law journal*, 18 (2) 375 - 383.

Hancock, R. & Mansfield, M. (2002) The Literacy Hour: a case for listening to children, *The Curriculum Journal*, 13 (2) 183–200.

Hannam, D. (2004) *Involving young people in identifying ways of gathering their views on the curriculum* London: QCA .

Harber, C. (2004) *Schooling as Violence*, Abingdon: RoutledgeFalmer.

Hartas, D. (2003) Pupil learning and world-views in citizenship, in L. Gearon (Ed.) *Learning to teach citizenship in the secondary school,* London: RoutledgeFalmer.

Heater, D. (2001) The history of citizenship education in England *The Curriculum Journal,* 12 (1) 103–123.

Hoffman, M.L. (1982) Development of prosocial motivation, empathy and guilt, in N. Mussen (Ed.) *The development of prosocial behaviour,* New York: Academic Press.

Hoffman, M.L. (1988) Moral development, in M.H. Borstein & M.E. Lamb (Eds.) *Developmental psychology: An advanced textbook,* Hillsdale NJ: Erlbaum.

Hoffman, J. (2004) *Citizenship beyond the state,* London: Sage.

Holt, J. (1969) *How children fail,* Harmondsworth: Penguin.

Horbury, H. & Pears, H. (1994) Collaborative Group-work: How Infant Children Can Manage it, *Education 3–13,* 22 (3) 20–28.

Huddleston, T. & Kerr, D. (2006) *Making sense of citizenship: A continuing professional development handbook,* London: Hodder Murray.

Huddleston, T & Rowe. D. (2003) Citizenship and the role of Language, in L. Gearon (Ed.) *Learning to teach citizenship in the secondary school,* London: RoutledgeFalmer.

Human Rights Watch (2001) *Scared at school: Sexual violence against girls in South African schools,* New York: Human Rights Watch.

Illich, I. (1971) *Deschooling society,* Harmondsworth: Penguin.

James, A., Jenks, C. & Prout, A. (2005) *Theorising childhood,* Cambridge: Polity Press.

James, W. (1890) *The principles of psychology,* New York: Henry Holt.

Johnson, D.W. & Johnson, R.T. (1989) *Cooperation and competition: theory and research,* Edina, Min: Interaction.

Johnson, D.W. & Johnson, R.T. (1994) Constructive Conflict in the Schools, *Journal of Social Issues,* 50 (1) 117–137.

Johnson, D.W. & Johnson, R.T. (1996) Conflict resolution and peer mediation programs in elementary and secondary schools: A review of the research, *Review of Educational Research,* 66 (4) 459–506.

Johnson, D.W., Johnson, R.T., Dudley, B., & Acikgoz, K. (1994) Effects of conflict resolution training on elementary school students, *Journal of Social Psychology,* 134 (6) 803–817.

Kahne, J. & Westheimer, J. (1996) In the service of what? The politics of service learning, *Phi-Delta Kappa,* 77, 9, 592–599.

Kerr, D. (2003) Citizenship: Local, National and International, in L. Gearon (Ed.) *Learning to teach citizenship in the secondary school,* London: RoutledgeFalmer .

Kerr, D. & Cleaver, E. (2004) *Citizenship education longitudinal study: Literature review – citizenship education one year on – what does it mean? Emerging definitions and approaches in the first year of national curriculum citizenship in England,* London: DfES.

Kingston Friends Workshop Group (1985) *Ways and Means: An approach to problem solving,* Kingston: Kingston Preparative Meeting.

Kohlberg, L. (1976) Moral stages in moralisation: The cognitive development approach, in T. Lickona (Ed.) *Moral development and behaviour: Theory, research and social issues,* New York: Holt Rinehart and Winston.

Kreidler, W.J. (1984) Creative conflict resolution: More than 200 activities for keeping peace in the classroom, London: Pearson Academic.

Krumm, V., Lamberger-Baumann, B. & Haider, G. (1997) Gewalt in der Schule: auch von Lehrern, *Empirische Pedagogik,* 11, 257–274.

Kyriacou, C. & Wan Chang, I. (1993) Mixing Different Types of Data and Approaches in Evaluating a Curriculum Package, *BERA Newsletter, Summer, 19–20.*

Lawrence, D. (1981) The development of a self-esteem questionnaire, *British Journal of Educational Psychology,* 51, 245–255.

Leggatt, A. (2001) *Tribunals for users: one system, one service: report of the review of tribunals,* London: Stationery Office.

Leimdorfer, T. (1990) Teaching creative responses to conflict, *New Era in Education,* 71 (2) 54–57.

Lewin, K. (1935) *A dynamic theory of personality,* New York: Macgraw-Hill.

Lewin, K. (1948) *Resolving Social Conflicts* Harper and Row, New York.

Liebmann, M. (2000) *Mediation in context,* London: Jessica Kingsley Publishers.

Lister, R. (2003) *Citizenship: feminist perspectives* (Basingstoke: Palgrave).

Lyon, J.M. (1991) Conflict resolution in an inner city middle school: An alternative approach, *School Counsellor,* 39 (2) 127–130.

MacBeathe, J. & Sugimine, H. (2003) *Self evaluation in the global classroom,* London: RoutledgeFalmer.

Mack, K. (2003) *Court Referral to ADR: Criteria and Research,* Melbourne: NADRAC/ AIJA.

Maines, B. & Robinson, G. (1988) *You can, you Know you can,* Bristol: Lucky Duck Publishing .

Maines, B. & Robinson, G. (1993) *Punishment: The milder the better,* Bristol: Lucky Duck Publishing.

Maines, B. & Robinson, G. (1994) *Managing Children: Managing themselves,* Bristol: Lucky Duck Publishing.

Marquand, D. (2004) *Decline of the public,* Cambridge: Polity Press.

Marshall, T. H. (1992 [1950]) Citizenship and social class. In T. H Marshall & T. Bottomore, *Citizenship and Social Class,* London: Pluto Press.

Martin, S.C. (1994) A preliminary evaluation of the adoption and implementation of assertive discipline at Robinson High School, *School organisation,* 14 (3) 321–330.

Masheder, M. (1986) *Let's Cooperate: activities and ideas for parents and teachers of young children for peaceful conflict solving.* London: Peace Education Project .

Maslow, A (1962) *Towards a Psychology of Being,* Princetown, N.J.: Van Nostrand.

Matthews, E. (1996) *Twentieth century French philosophy*, Oxford: Oxford University Press.

McCold, P. (2003) *Evaluation of a Restorative Milieu: CSF Buxmont School / Day Treatment Programs 1999–2001*, Paper presented at the Second International Conference on Violence in Schools, Quebec City, Canada, 2003.

McConnell, J. (1992) *The Friend*, 29th May, London: Quaker Home Service.

McMahon, C. (1997) Conflict Resolution Network Schools Australia, *European Journal of Intercultural Studies*, 8 (2) 169–184.

McNamara, K. (1996) "Say NO to bullying!": a message from your peers, *Pastoral Care in Education*, 14 (2) 16–20.

Meadows, S. (1988) Piaget's contribution to understanding cognitive development: An assessment for the late 1980s, in K. Richardson & S. Sheldon (Eds.) *Cognitive development to adolescence*, Buckingham: Open University Press.

Mediation UK (2006) Website: http://www.mediationuk.org.uk/.

Melling, R. & Swinson, J. (1995) Assertive discipline: Four wheels on this wagon – a reply to Robinson and Maines, *Educational psychology in practice*, 11 (3) 3–8.

Miller, R.W. (1993) In Search of Peace, *Schools in the Middle*, 2, 3.

Mooij, T. (1994) *Violence in secondary education*, Nijmegen: Catholic University, Institute for Applied Social Science.

Moore, C.M. (1994) Why do we mediate? in J.P. Folger & T.S. Jones (Eds.) *New directions in mediation: Communication research and perspectives*, California: Sage.

Moore, B.S. & Eisenberg, N. (1984) The development of altruism. In G Whitehurst (Ed.) *Annals of child development*, Greenwich CT: JAI Press.

Morrison, K. (2002) *School leadership and complexity theory*, London: RoutledgeFalmer.

Morrison, B. (2003) Regulating safe school communities: being responsive and restorative, *Journal of Educational Administration*, 4 (6) 689–704 .

Moseley, J. (1994) *Turn your school around, Wisbech Cambridge: LDA* .

National Curriculum Council (1989) *Teaching Talking and Learning in Key Stage Three, London:* National Oracy Project.

NADRAC (1997) *Alternative dispute resolution definitions*, March 1997, Canberra: NADRAC. .

NADRAC (2003) *Dispute Resolution Terms: the use of terms in (alternative) dispute resolution*, Canberra: NADRAC.

Neill, S.R. St. J. (2001) *Unacceptable Pupil behaviour: A survey analysed for the National Union of Teachers*, Warwick: University of Warwick.

Noddings, N. (2003) *Caring: A feminine approach to ethics and moral education*, Berkeley: University of California .

Nowicki, S. & Strickland, B. (1973) A Locus of Control Scale for Children, *Journal of Consulting and Clinical Psychology*, 40, 30–36.

Ofsted (2005) *Citizenship in secondary schools: evidence from Ofsted inspections* (2003/04) London: Ofsted.

Olweus, D. (1999) Sweden, in P.K. Smith, Y Morita, J. Junger-Tas, D. Olweus, R. Catalano and P. Slee (Eds.) *The Nature of School Bullying: a cross-national perspective.* London & New York: RoutledgeFalmer.

Ortega, R., Del Rey, R. & Fernandez, I. (2003) Working together to prevent school violence, in P.K. Smith (Ed.) *Violence in schools: the response in Europe,* London: Routledgefalmer.

Osler, A. (2003) The Crick report and the future of multiethnic Britain, in L. Gearon (Ed.) *Learning to teach citizenship in the secondary school,* London: RoutledgeFalmer .

Osler, A. & Starkey, H. (2005) *Changing citizenship: Democracy and inclusion in education,* Buckingham: Open University Press.

Parlett, M & Hamilton, D. (1972) Evaluation as illumination: A new approach to the study of innovatory programmes. In R. Murphy, and H. Torrance, (Eds) *Evaluating Education: Issues and methods.* Milton Keynes: Open University.

Pattie, C., Seyd, P. & Whiteley, P. (2004) *Citizenship in Britain: values, participation and democracy,* Cambridge: Cambridge University Press.

Piaget, J. (1950) *The psychology of intelligence,* New York: Harcourt.

Plowden (1968) *Children and their primary schools: A report of the central advisory council for education,* London: HMSO.

Plummer, K. (2003) *Intimate citizenship: private decisions and public dialogues,* Washington: University of Washington Press.

Pollard, A. & Triggs, P. (2000) *What Pupils Say, Changing Policy and Practice in Primary Education,* London, Continuum.

Porter, G. (1995) Organisation of schooling: Achieving access and quality through inclusion, *Prospects,* 25 (2) 299–309.

Powell, S.D. & Makin, M. (1994) Enabling Pupils with Learning Difficulties to Reflect on Their Own Thinking, *British Educational Research Journal,* 20 (5) 579–593.

Prutzman, P. (1988) *The Friendly Classroom for a Small Planet,* Philadelphia: New Society Publishers.

Riley, K & Rustique-Forrester, E (2002) *Working with Disaffected Students: Why students lose interest in school and what we can do about it,* London: Paul Chapman Publishing.

Roberts, M. (1994) *Skills for Self-managed Learning: Autonomous learning by research projects.* Derby: Education Now Publishing Cooperative .

Robinson, G. & Maines, B. (1995) Assertive discipline: No wheels on your wagon: A reply to Swinson and Melling, *Educational psychology in practice,* 11 (3) 9–11.

Rogers, C. & Freiberg, H.J. (1994) *Freedom to learn,* New York: Macmillan.

Rogers, C.R. (1951) *Client-centred Therapy,* Boston: Houghton Mifflin.

Rogers, B. (1996) Mediation has certainly worked for us, *Education and Health,* 14 (1) 1–4.

Rorty, R. (1979) *Philosophy and the mirror of nature,* Princeton: Princeton University Press.

Ruddock, P. (2004) Towards a less litigious Australia: the Australian government's ADR initiatives, *The Arbitrator and Mediator* 23 (1) 1–11 .

Ruddock, J. & Flutter, J. (2004) *How to improve your school: Giving pupils a voice,* London: Continuum Books.

Rustemier, S. & Vaughan, M. (2005) *Are LEAs in England abandoning inclusive education?* Bristol: CSIE.

Samuels, A. (2001) *Politics on the couch: citizenship and the internal life,* London: Profile Books.

Sandy, S.V. & Cochran, K.M. (1998) *Peaceful kids (ECSEL): Conflict resolution skills for pre-school children (programme guide)* New York: International Centre for Cooperation and Conflict Resolution.

Sandy, S.V. and Cochran, K.M. (2000) The development of conflict resolution skills in children: Preschool to adolescence, in M. Deutsch, & P.T. Coleman (2000) *The Handbook of Conflict Resolution: Theory and Practice,* San Francisco: Jossey-Bass.

Sartre, J. P. (2000/1943) *Being and nothingness.* London: Routledge .

Schaps, E. & Solomon, D. (1990) Schools and classrooms as caring communities, *Educational leadership,* 48 (3) 38–42.

Schofield, J.W. (1993) Increasing the generalizability of qualitative research. In M Hammersley (Ed.) *Educational Research: Current issues,* Buckingham: Open University Press.

Schon, D.A. (1991) *The reflective practitioner: How professionals think in action,* Aldershot: Avebury.

Sebastiao, J., Campos, J. & Tomas de Almeida, A. (2003) Portugal: The gap between the political agenda and local initiatives, in P.K. Smith (Ed.) *Violence in schools: the response in Europe,* London: Routledgefalmer.

Sellman, E. (2002) Peer mediation, school culture and sustainability, *Pastoral care,* June, 7–11.

Selman, R.L. (1980) *The growth of interpersonal understanding,* New York: Academic Press.

Sharp, S. Peer-led approaches to care, *Pastoral Care in Education,* December, 21–24.

Smith, P.K. (2003) *Violence in schools: the response in Europe,* London: Routledgefalmer.

Southwark Mediation Centre (1993) *Annual Report,* Available from Southwark Mediation Centre, Southwark, London, UK.

Spencer, D. (2005) *Essential Dispute Resolution,* Coogee NSW: Cavendish Publishing.

Stacey, H. (2001) *Learning How to Mediate,* London: Sage Publications.

Stacey, H. & Robinson, P. (1997) *Let's Mediate: A teacher's guide to peer support and conflict resolution skills for all ages.* London: Sage Publications .

Stacey, H., Robinson, P., & Cremin, D. (1997) Using Conflict Resolution and Peer Mediation to Tackle Bullying, in D.P Tattum, & D.A. Lane (Eds.) *Bullying Home School and Community.* London: David Fulton Publishers.

Stenhouse, L. (1975) *An introduction to curriculum research and development*, London: Heinemann.

Stenhouse, L. (1987) The conduct, analysis and reporting of case study in educational research and evaluation, in R. Murphy and H. Torrance (Eds) *Evaluating Education: Issues and methods*. Buckingham: Open University Press.

Stuart, L.A. (1991) *Conflict Resolution Using Mediation Skills in the Elementary Schools*. Report available from the Conflict Manager Programme, Virginia, United States.

Tattum, D.P. & Lane D.A. (1997) *Bullying Home School and Community*. London: David Fulton Publishers.

Taylor, M. (2003) *Going round in circles: implementing and learning from Circle Time*, Slough: NFER.

Taylor, C., Fitz, J & Gorard, S. (2005) Diversity, specialisation and equity in education, *Oxford Review of Education*, 31 (1) 47–70 .

Taylor Nelson AGB (1995) *Civil law and the public* London: National Consumer Council.

Tesler, P. (2001) *Collaborative Law: Achieving Effective Resolution in Divorce Without Litigation*, Chicago, Illinois USA: American Bar Association. .

Thomas, G. Walker, D. & Webb, J. (1998) *The making of the inclusive school*, London: Routledge.

Thomas, G. & Loxley ,A. (2001) *Deconstructing Special Education and Constructing Inclusion*, Buckingham: Open University Press .

Thomas, G. & Vaughan, M. (2004) *Inclusive Education: Readings and reflections*, Buckingham: Open University Press.

Thompson, S. (1996) Peer mediation - a peaceful solution, *School-Counselor*, 44 (2) 151–154. .

Topping, K. (1996) Reaching where adults cannot: peer education and peer counselling, *Educational Psychology in Practice,*11(4) 23–29.

Torney-Purta, J., Lehmann, R., Oswald, H. & Shulz, W. (2001) *Citizenship and education in twenty-eight countries: Civic knowledge and participation at age fourteen*, Amsterdam: International Association for the Evaluation of Educational Achievement.

Turiel, E. (1966) An experimental test of the sequentiality of developmental stages in the child's moral judgements, *Journal of personality and social psychology*, 3, 611–618.

Tyrrell, J. & Farrell, S. (1995) *Peer Mediation in Primary Schools*. Belfast: University of Ulster, Vulliamy, G. (1990) The potential of qualitative educational research in developing countries. In G.Vulliamy, K. Lewin, & D. Stevens, *Doing Educational Research in Developing Countries*, London: Falmer .

Warne, A. (2003) Establishing peer mediation in a special school context, *Pastoral care*, December 2003, 27–33.

Waterhouse, P. (1983) *Supported Self-Study in Secondary Education*. London: CET.

Webb, A. & Kaye, P. (1996) "A little help from my friends": a secondary school peer support programme, *Pastoral Care in Education*, 14 (2) 21–25.

White, M. (1991) *Self Esteem: Promoting Positive Practices for Responsible Behaviour, Circle Time Strategies for Schools*, Cambridge: Daniels Publishing .

Whitty, G. (2002) *Making Sense of Education Policy*, London: Paul Chapman.

Woolf, L. (1996) *Access to Justice: the final report to the Lord Chancellor on the Civil Justice System in England and Wales*, London: Stationery Office.

Index